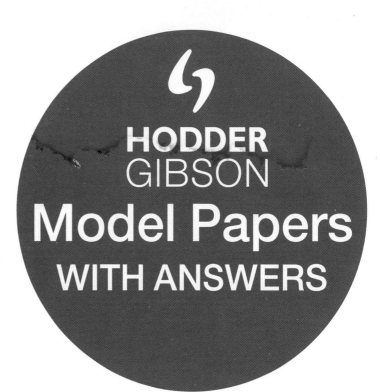

HODDER GIBSON

Model Papers

WITH ANSWERS

PLUS: Official SQA Specimen Paper
& 2015 Past Paper With Answers

Higher for CfE
Computing Science

2014 Specimen Question Paper,
Model Papers & 2015 Exam

HODDER
GIBSON
AN HACHETTE UK COMPANY

This book contains the official 2014 SQA Specimen Question Paper and 2015 Exam for Higher for CfE Computing Science, with associated SQA approved answers modified from the official marking instructions that accompany the paper.

In addition the book contains model papers, together with answers, plus study skills advice. These papers, some of which may include a limited number of previously published SQA questions, have been specially commissioned by Hodder Gibson, and have been written by experienced senior teachers and examiners in line with the new Higher for CfE syllabus and assessment outlines, Spring 2014. This is not SQA material but has been devised to provide further practice for Higher for CfE examinations in 2015 and beyond.

Hodder Gibson is grateful to the copyright holders, as credited on the final page of the Answer Section, for permission to use their material. Every effort has been made to trace the copyright holders and to obtain their permission for the use of copyright material. Hodder Gibson will be happy to receive information allowing us to rectify any error or omission in future editions.

Hachette UK's policy is to use papers that are natural, renewable and recyclable products and made from wood grown in sustainable forests. The logging and manufacturing processes are expected to conform to the environmental regulations of the country of origin.

Orders: please contact Bookpoint Ltd, 130 Park Drive, Milton Park, Abingdon, Oxon OX14 4SE. Telephone: (44) 01235 827720. Fax: (44) 01235 400454. Lines are open 9.00–5.00, Monday to Saturday, with a 24-hour message answering service. Visit our website at www.hoddereducation.co.uk. Hodder Gibson can be contacted direct on: Tel: 0141 848 1609; Fax: 0141 889 6315; email: hoddergibson@hodder.co.uk

This collection first published in 2015 by
Hodder Gibson, an imprint of Hodder Education,
An Hachette UK Company
2a Christie Street
Paisley PA1 1NB

Typeset by Aptara, Inc.

Printed in the UK

A catalogue record for this title is available from the British Library

ISBN: 978-1-4718-6072-0

3 2 1

2016 2015

Introduction

Study Skills – what you need to know to pass exams!

Pause for thought

Many students might skip quickly through a page like this. After all, we all know how to revise. Do you really though?

Think about this:

"IF YOU ALWAYS DO WHAT YOU ALWAYS DO, YOU WILL ALWAYS GET WHAT YOU HAVE ALWAYS GOT."

Do you like the grades you get? Do you want to do better? If you get full marks in your assessment, then that's great! Change nothing! This section is just to help you get that little bit better than you already are.

There are two main parts to the advice on offer here. The first part highlights fairly obvious things but which are also very important. The second part makes suggestions about revision that you might not have thought about but which WILL help you.

Part 1

DOH! It's so obvious but …

Start revising in good time

Don't leave it until the last minute – this will make you panic.

Make a revision timetable that sets out work time AND play time.

Sleep and eat!

Obvious really, and very helpful. Avoid arguments or stressful things too – even games that wind you up. You need to be fit, awake and focused!

Know your place!

Make sure you know exactly **WHEN and WHERE** your exams are.

Know your enemy!

Make sure you know what to expect in the exam.

How is the paper structured?

How much time is there for each question?

What types of question are involved?

Which topics seem to come up time and time again?

Which topics are your strongest and which are your weakest?

Are all topics compulsory or are there choices?

Learn by DOING!

There is no substitute for past papers and practice papers – they are simply essential! Tackling this collection of papers and answers is exactly the right thing to be doing as your exams approach.

Part 2

People learn in different ways. Some like low light, some bright. Some like early morning, some like evening / night. Some prefer warm, some prefer cold. But everyone uses their BRAIN and the brain works when it is active. Passive learning – sitting gazing at notes – is the most INEFFICIENT way to learn anything. Below you will find tips and ideas for making your revision more effective and maybe even more enjoyable. What follows gets your brain active, and active learning works!

Activity 1 – Stop and review

Step 1

When you have done no more than 5 minutes of revision reading STOP!

Step 2

Write a heading in your own words which sums up the topic you have been revising.

Step 3

Write a summary of what you have revised in no more than two sentences. Don't fool yourself by saying, "I know it, but I cannot put it into words". That just means you don't know it well enough. If you cannot write your summary, revise that section again, knowing that you must write a summary at the end of it. Many of you will have notebooks full of blue/black ink writing. Many of the pages will not be especially attractive or memorable so try to liven them up a bit with colour as you are reviewing and rewriting. **This is a great memory aid, and memory is the most important thing.**

Activity 2 – Use technology!

Why should everything be written down? Have you thought about "mental" maps, diagrams, cartoons and colour to help you learn? And rather than write down notes, why not record your revision material?

What about having a text message revision session with friends? Keep in touch with them to find out how and what they are revising and share ideas and questions.

Why not make a video diary where you tell the camera what you are doing, what you think you have learned and what you still have to do? No one has to see or hear it, but the process of having to organise your thoughts in a formal way to explain something is a very important learning practice.

Be sure to make use of electronic files. You could begin to summarise your class notes. Your typing might be slow, but it will get faster and the typed notes will be easier to read than the scribbles in your class notes. Try to add different fonts and colours to make your work stand out. You can easily Google relevant pictures, cartoons and diagrams which you can copy and paste to make your work more attractive and **MEMORABLE**.

Activity 3 – This is it. Do this and you will know lots!

Step 1

In this task you must be very honest with yourself! Find the SQA syllabus for your subject (www.sqa.org.uk). Look at how it is broken down into main topics called MANDATORY knowledge. That means stuff you MUST know.

Step 2

BEFORE you do ANY revision on this topic, write a list of everything that you already know about the subject. It might be quite a long list but you only need to write it once. It shows you all the information that is already in your long-term memory so you know what parts you do not need to revise!

Step 3

Pick a chapter or section from your book or revision notes. Choose a fairly large section or a whole chapter to get the most out of this activity.

With a buddy, use Skype, Facetime, Twitter or any other communication you have, to play the game "If this is the answer, what is the question?". For example, if you are revising Geography and the answer you provide is "meander", your buddy would have to make up a question like "What is the word that describes a feature of a river where it flows slowly and bends often from side to side?".

Make up 10 "answers" based on the content of the chapter or section you are using. Give this to your buddy to solve while you solve theirs.

Step 4

Construct a wordsearch of at least 10 × 10 squares. You can make it as big as you like but keep it realistic. Work together with a group of friends. Many apps allow you to make wordsearch puzzles online. The words and phrases can go in any direction and phrases can be split. Your puzzle must only contain facts linked to the topic you are revising. Your task is to find 10 bits of information to hide in your puzzle, but you must not repeat information that you used in Step 3. DO NOT show where the words are. Fill up empty squares with random letters. Remember to keep a note of where your answers are hidden but do not show your friends. When you have a complete puzzle, exchange it with a friend to solve each other's puzzle.

Step 5

Now make up 10 questions (not "answers" this time) based on the same chapter used in the previous two tasks. Again, you must find NEW information that you have not yet used. Now it's getting hard to find that new information! Again, give your questions to a friend to answer.

Step 6

As you have been doing the puzzles, your brain has been actively searching for new information. Now write a NEW LIST that contains only the new information you have discovered when doing the puzzles. Your new list is the one to look at repeatedly for short bursts over the next few days. Try to remember more and more of it without looking at it. After a few days, you should be able to add words from your second list to your first list as you increase the information in your long-term memory.

FINALLY! Be inspired...

Make a list of different revision ideas and beside each one write **THINGS I HAVE** tried, **THINGS I WILL** try and **THINGS I MIGHT** try. Don't be scared of trying something new.

And remember – "FAIL TO PREPARE AND PREPARE TO FAIL!"

Higher Computing Science

The course

Although you may have passed National 5 Computing Science, it is important to understand that the step up to Higher is demanding and may require a different approach to ensure your success. To understand a course at Higher level often requires that you fully understand one fact before you move on to the next. If you leave a lesson confused, do something about it. Read over your notes again in the evening, ask your teacher for further explanation, attend study groups, use the world wide web for research or ask your friends for help. Whichever route you take, make sure that you get into this habit early on in the year.

The exam

The new Higher Computing Science course has a question paper which contains two sections and 90 marks (60% of the total mark). Approximately 50% of the marks will be awarded for questions related to *Software Design and Development*, and 50% to *Information Systems Design and Development*.

Candidates will complete the question paper in 2 hours.

Section 1 will have 20 marks and will consist of short answer questions assessing breadth of knowledge from across both Units. Most questions will have 1–2 marks.

Section 2 will have 70 marks and will consist of approximately 6–8 extended response questions, each with approximately 8–12 marks. Questions will be of a problem-solving nature rather than direct recall and will include extended descriptions and explanations.

Approximately 50% of the marks will be awarded for questions related to *Software Design and Development*. These will include questions from the following areas:

- computational constructs and concepts
- explaining code
- writing code
- standard algorithms
- data types and structures
- software development – design, testing, documentation
- types of languages
- low level operations and computer architecture.

Questions related to programming will use the form of 'pseudocode' below:

Variable types: INTEGER, REAL, BOOLEAN, CHARACTER

Structured types: ARRAY, STRING, RECORD

Subprogram: PROCUDURE, FUNCTION

System entities: DISPLAY, KEYBOARD

Assignment: SET … TO …

Conditions: IF .. THEN .. (ELSE) … END IF

Conditional repetition: WHILE … DO … END WHILE
REPEAT … UNTIL …

Fixed repetition: REPEAT … TIMES … END REPEAT

Iteration: FOR .. FROM .. TO .. DO .. END FOR
FOR EACH … FROM … DO … END FOR EACH

Input/output: RECEIVE … FROM … ,
SEND … TO … , OPEN, CLOSE, CREATE

Operations: -, +, *, /, ^, mod, &

Comparisons: =, ≠, <, <=, >, >=

Logical operators: AND, OR, NOT

Pre-defined functions: id(parameters)

If you are required to write in code then you can use any programming language with which you are familiar or write your answer in pseudocode.

Approximately 50% of the marks will be awarded for questions related to *Information System Design and Development*. These will include questions from the following areas:

- database design, structures, links and operations
- client-side and server-side coding (including HTML, CSS and Javascript)
- website design, structures and links
- coding
- media types (including file size calculations)
- information system development – purpose, features, user interface, testing
- technical implementation – hardware, software, storage, networking/connectivity
- security, legal and environmental issues.

Question types

The Computing Science exam comprises two question types:

1. Knowledge & Understanding – questions that simply ask you to write down or explain a fact or skill you have learned.
2. Problem Solving – questions where you are required to apply your knowledge to an unfamiliar scenario.

KU questions can be easily prepared for by simply memorising lots of facts. PS questions require practice. Unseen exam questions will go some way towards preparing you for PS questions but you may find that you quickly run out of new examples. Try making up your own question scenarios and swap them with a friend. Write your own programs or create a database of your own, query it and create a variety of reports from the data. You'll find that the task of making up the questions or scenarios in a problem solving context is an exercise in itself.

General advice

Remember to read the questions carefully and answer what is being asked.

Trade Names

It is never acceptable to use a company name in an answer such as Microsoft Access, Serif Web-Plus, etc. Use the generic terms such as Databases, Web-Design packages.

Conversion

If you are asked to convert a number into an 8-bit binary number make sure that your answer has 8 bits!

Technical Terminology

It is important that the correct technical terminology is used, e.g. USB Flash Drive – not USB pen, USB stick, Pen Drive or other commonly used expressions.

Units

Remember there are 1024 bytes in a Kilobyte not 1000.

- 1024 Kilobytes in a Megabyte
- 1024 Megabytes in a Gigabyte
- 1024 Gigabytes in a Terabyte

Data Structure

The data structures you are required to know at Higher are one-dimensional arrays, records and sequential files.

Memory

Many candidates confuse the RAM memory with Backing Storage. Remember RAM memory is used to store programs and data temporarily while the program is being used. The Backing Storage is used to hold programs and data permanently until you are ready to use them. When you open an application it is taken from the Backing Storage (e.g. Hard Disc Drive) and placed into RAM memory.

Technical Implementation

Use your common sense when thinking about the reasons why you would choose a particular type of hardware. Does it have to be portable? Does it require fast processing? What is the most sensible storage device? What is the best networking solution for this particular task?

Calculating Storage Requirements

When calculating the storage requirements for photographs too many candidates forget that DPI must be squared. Remember to multiply the number of bits required to store the colour – NOT the number of colours!

For example, an image measures 3 inches by 4 inches and has a resolution of 600dpi in 8 colours

= 3 x 4 x 600 x 600 x 3 (3 bits can give 8 combinations)
= 12960000 bits = 12960000/8 =1620000 bytes
= 1620000/1024 = 1582.03 Kb = 1882.03Kb / 1024
= 1.54 Mb.

Storage Devices and Cloud Storage

Candidates often confuse the three main types of storage devices.

- Magnetic – Hard Disk Drives, Floppy Disc Drives, Magnetic Tape (DAT)
- Solid State – USB Flash Drives, Solid State Hard Drives
- Optical – CD-ROM, CD-R, CD-RW, DVD-ROM, DVD-R, DVD-RW and Blu-Ray

Computers and the Law

Candidates must give the correct, full names of the appropriate laws such as the "Regulation of Investigatory Powers Act", "Computer Misuse Act", "Communications Act" and "Copyright, Design and Patents Act".

Interfaces

Many candidates forget why an interface is required. Remember an interface changes electrical voltages, changes analogue to digital, buffers data and deals with control signals.

Pre-Defined Functions

Remember that pre-defined functions are built-in sections of code that have been written and tested and are available for programmers to use. They include common functions such as Random numbers and Rounding.

Cloud – Private, Public, Hybrid

Ensure you can accurately explain the need for three types of cloud storage by describing uses of each.

Standard Algorithms

Make sure that you have a good understanding and are able to code the five standard algorithms required at Higher.

- Input Validation
- Find Maximum
- Find Minimum
- Count Occurrences
- Linear Search

Good luck!

The most pleasing results for teachers are not necessarily the students who get the A pass. It's often the students who achieve their potential, even if that is just scraping a pass. Every year teachers see a few pupils who "could have done better". Don't let that be you!

Remember that the rewards for passing Higher Computing Science are well worth it! Your pass will help you get the future you want for yourself. In the exam, be confident in your own ability. If you're not sure how to answer a question, trust your instincts and give it a go anyway, or move on quickly. Working at a reasonable pace will allow time to return to unanswered questions later. Finally, keep calm and don't panic! GOOD LUCK!

2014 Specimen Question Paper

National
Qualifications
SPECIMEN ONLY

Mark

SQ09/H/01

Computing Science

Date — Not applicable

Duration — 2 hours

Fill in these boxes and read what is printed below.

Full name of centre

Town

Forename(s)

Surname

Number of seat

Date of birth

Day	Month	Year
D D	M M	Y Y

Scottish candidate number

Total marks — 90

SECTION 1 — 20 marks

Attempt ALL questions.

SECTION 2 — 70 marks

Attempt ALL questions.

Show all workings.

Write your answers clearly in the spaces provided in this booklet. Additional space for answers is provided at the end of this booket. If you use this space you must clearly identify the question number you are attempting.

Use **blue** or **black** ink.

Before leaving the examination room you must give this booklet to the Invigilator; if you do not, you may lose all the marks for this paper.

SQA
©

MARKS | DO NOT WRITE IN THIS MARGIN

SECTION 1 — 20 marks

Attempt ALL questions

1. (a) A company is developing a new software package. State when the company would use beta testing.

1

_____

_____

(b) State **two** reasons why the client should be involved in the testing.

2

_____

_____

_____

_____

2. Clare has just started programming and has created an algorithm to search the array `cars` which holds one hundred car registration numbers.

Clare wishes to search for a specific registration number each time she uses the program. Clare's algorithm is shown below.

```
line
1       SET check TO 0
2       SET counter TO 1
3       RECEIVE registration FROM KEYBOARD
4       REPEAT
5           IF cars[counter] = registration THEN
6               SET check TO 1
7           END IF
8           SET counter TO counter + 1
9       UNTIL check = 1 OR counter = 101
```

Clare could have used a Boolean variable called "found" as part of this algorithm. She alters line 1 to read:

```
1       SET found TO false
```

MARKS | DO NOT WRITE IN THIS MARGIN

2. **(continued)**

With reference to the line numbers shown, state the other changes that Clare would need to make if she wished to use this Boolean variable.   **2**

3. Jade is writing a program on her PC that is intended to run on her mobile phone.

Explain why an emulator is required in the programming environment.   **2**

4. Scottish Airways operate a real-time booking system. To ensure the security of the data they make a daily backup of the whole system.

Explain what additional backups would be required to ensure no loss of data in the event of a system failure.   **2**

MARKS | DO NOT WRITE IN THIS MARGIN

5. SN is a software development company. They have been invited to bid for the contract to develop software for a multinational supermarket chain.

   (a) Explain why using a rapid application development (RAD) methodology could be beneficial to SN when bidding for the contract.

2

_____

_____

_____

_____

   (b) Describe how Agile methodologies could be used in the effective production of the software.

2

_____

_____

_____

_____

6. A programming language uses 32 bits to represent real numbers such as the negative value -0.000000016.

Explain how the 32 bits could be allocated to store such numbers.

3

_____

_____

_____

_____

_____

MARKS | DO NOT WRITE IN THIS MARGIN

7. A section of code has been written to total the contents of an array of 100 values.

```
line
1      SET total TO 0
2      FOR index FROM 1 TO 100
3              SET total TO total + values[index]
4      END FOR
```

(a) Explain why a compiler may be more efficient than an interpreter in the execution of this code.

    2

_____

_____

_____

_____

_____

(b) Explain the benefit of this code being present in cache memory.

    2

_____

_____

_____

_____

MARKS | DO NOT WRITE IN THIS MARGIN

SECTION 2 — 70 marks

Attempt ALL questions

1. A program has been written to find the **position** of the maximum value in a list, however the program stops responding. The algorithm responsible is shown below.

```
line
1     SET source TO [71,76,66,67,89,72]
2     SET position TO 1
3     FOR counter FROM 2 TO 6
4            IF source[counter]>source[position] THEN
5                 SET counter TO position
6            END IF
7     END FOR
```

(a) Line 1 shows the use of a 1-D array to store the list of values, instead of six individual variables. Describe **two** advantages of using a 1-D array to store this list of values.

2

_____

_____

_____

_____

(b) A trace table is being used to record the changes to variables when stepping through the code.

(Line 4 does not change a variable's value and so is not included.)

Line	Source	Position	Counter
1	[77,66,88,67,89,72]		
2			
3			
5			

(i) Complete the information in the table above, recording the value assigned to the variable for line numbers 2, 3 and 5.

3

MARKS | DO NOT WRITE IN THIS MARGIN

1. (b) (continued)

(ii) Explain why the loop never terminates.   **2**

_____

_____

_____

_____

(iii) Describe how the algorithm should be corrected.   **2**

_____

_____

_____

_____

(iv) The program stopped responding because the loop did not terminate. This is an example of an execution error. Describe another type of error that can occur when a program runs.   **2**

_____

_____

_____

_____

(c) Describe how a feature of the software development environment could have been used to locate the area of code with the error.   **2**

_____

_____

_____

_____

Total marks   13

2. CheckTax have developed a function to return the taxcode (A, B, C or D) that should be used for an employee's pay. The function is to be used for employees that have income from two different sources. For example:

Combined income	Taxcode
Less than 9000	A
9000 and over (but less than 43000)	B
43000 and over (but less than 60000)	C
60000 and over	D

The inputs and output of this function are show in the diagram below.

The function was developed using the following algorithm to determine a taxcode for any value of total income.

```
line

1     SET taxcode TO "Z"

2     SET salary TO (income1 + income2)

3     IF salary < 9000 THEN

4             SET taxcode TO "A"

5     END IF

6     IF salary > 9000 AND salary < 43000 THEN

7             SET taxcode TO "B"

8     END IF

9     IF salary > 43000 AND salary < 60000 THEN

10            SET taxcode TO "C"

11    END IF

12    IF salary > 60000 THEN

13            SET taxcode TO "D"

14    END IF

15    RETURN taxcode
```

MARKS | DO NOT WRITE IN THIS MARGIN

2. **(continued)**

(a) Explain why this algorithm would return an incorrect taxcode if income1 is 30000 and income2 is 30000.

2

_____

_____

_____

_____

(b) The lead programmer comments that the use of a series of IF statements is inefficient.

Using pseudocode or a language with which you are familiar, rewrite the algorithm to correct the logic error and make the code more efficient.

3

MARKS | DO NOT WRITE IN THIS MARGIN

2. (continued)

(c) Jeanette works for a bank and has downloaded the corrected function, `taxcode`, from CheckTax's online library. Bank employees receive an annual salary and bonus pay and Jeanette's program stores these values in variables `salary` and `bonus`. It also stores the employee's tax code in a variable called `code`.

Using pseudocode or a language with which you are familiar, write an algorithm for a subroutine that will:

•   Ask the user for the values for variables `salary` and `bonus`
•   Use the function to assign the variable `code`
•   Display `code` on screen   3

(d) Jeanette has commissioned CheckTax to create some software for the bank. Part of the software will be designed for a web-based system. CheckTax have decided to use wire-framing as part of the design process.

Describe **two** factors that CheckTax will have to consider while using wire-framing.   2

MARKS

3. The weather statistics are recorded for each day of the 30 days of November. For each day, the statistics recorded include the rainfall in millimetres and the lowest temperature. Some of the data is shown below.

Day		Rainfall		Lowest temperature
1		12		8
2		5		4
3		0		-3
4		5		1
5		0		-4
. . .		. . .		. . .
30		21		6

(a) The rainfall figures are held in an array called `rainfall` and the lowest temperatures in an array called `lowtemp`. Using pseudocode or a language with which you are familiar, write an algorithm to count the number of dry days below freezing and write this number of days to a text file called `drydays`.

5

MARKS | DO NOT WRITE IN THIS MARGIN

3. **(continued)**

(b) The algorithm used to count the number of dry days below freezing is implemented as a subroutine. Describe how the subroutine could make this value available to other parts of the program.

1

_____

_____

_____

_____

MARKS | DO NOT WRITE IN THIS MARGIN

4. Homeview is an estate agent which specialises in the sale of residential properties in Aberdeenshire. It uses a dynamic database-driven website to display the range of properties it has for sale. Details of each property are held within a relational database.

(a) Describe **two** reasons why a dynamic database-driven website is a benefit for site visitors.

2

(b) The managing director of Homeview wants to update the website and change the appearance of the text throughout all the web pages. He instructs his technical staff to make the following changes using cascading style sheets (CSS).

Text	Font	Size	Colour	Style
Headings	Verdana	20	Black	Bold
Sub Headings	Tahoma	16	Red	Bold
Body Text	Arial	12	Blue	Regular

Create a CSS rule that will implement the changes for the Sub Headings.

3

4. (continued)

(c) To gain access to more detailed property information, users must complete a registration form to create a unique username and password.

Describe **one** example of input validation that could be applied to a **username** when it is first registered.

1

_____

_____

_____

(d) When registering, the user must enter a valid e-mail address. This validation process is carried out by code written in a scripting language.

In the language used, the syntax for an IF statement is:

```
if (expression)
{
    command(s)
}
```

and the OR comparator is written using the symbol ||

The following code is used to validate the e-mail address:

```
if (atpos<2 || dotpos<atpos+2 || dotpos+2>=length)
{
    alert("Not a valid e-mail address");
    return false;
}
```

In the code above:

- the variable `length` stores the number of characters in the e-mail address
- the variable `atpos` stores the position of the @ character
- the variable `dotpos` stores the position of the last dot

For example, if the e-mail address is myname@sqa.com
then `length` = 14, `atpos` = 7 and `dotpos` = 11

Explain how the code above would process the validation of the e-mail address: my.name@net

3

MARKS | DO NOT WRITE IN THIS MARGIN

5. Choose a contemporary development in intelligent systems.

(a) Briefly describe the main features of this development.   2

(b) Describe **one** beneficial economic impact of this development.   1

(c) Describe **one** problem that this development might cause for society.   1

6. Dog Walkers is a company that walks dogs when their owners are at work.

The company has a database to store details of the dogs, their owners and the walkers. The data is stored in the following tables.

Dog	Owner	Walk	Walker
Dog ID	Owner ID	Walk ID	Walker ID
Dog name	Owner name	Dog ID*	Walker name
Dog type	Owner address	Walker ID*	Walker phone number
Gender	Owner phone	No. of days per week	
Walks well with others		Cost	
Photo			
Owner ID*			

(a) State **two** one-to-many relationships that exist between the tables.   2

_____

_____

_____

_____

6.   (continued)

The following form is used to enter each dog's details.

Dog walkers

Dog name	Buster
Dog type	Golden Labrador
Gender	Male
Walks well with others	Yes
Photo	
Owner ID*	123

(b)   Describe **two** ways of improving the usability of this form.

2

_____

_____

_____

_____

6. **(continued)**

(c) The following is produced for a walker.

Walker: Susan			
Dog name	**Dog type**	**Owner address**	**Walks well with others**
Bertie	Basset Hound	6 Flower Way	Yes
Buster	Golden Labrador	103 Mayflower	Yes
Goldie	Spaniel	65 Varley Road	Yes
Ralph	German Shepherd	The Drive	Yes

Describe how the company would use the database software to produce this report.

5

MARKS | DO NOT WRITE IN THIS MARGIN

7. WebGo develop websites for mobile devices. WebGo have developed a site for a new university.

   (a) The university would like the website to incorporate an internal search engine. Search engines make use of crawler software.

   Describe **two** ways that WebGo could ensure that the new website was optimised for indexing by crawler software.

   2

   (b) Students have reported issues with one of the web pages that is returned following a search.

   The web page is supposed to display images of the student union gym and cafeteria. When the page loads the images appear as follows.

   ☒ img24535

   Explain how the HTML code could be changed to make this web page more accessible in the event of images not appearing on screen.

   2

MARKS | DO NOT WRITE IN THIS MARGIN

7. (continued)

(c) The university has a web page devoted to foreign exchange students. As part of this web page there is an image of a national flag. The image can be compressed using a lossless compression technique.

Explain why lossless compression results in a significant reduction in the file size for this image.

2

MARKS | DO NOT WRITE IN THIS MARGIN

8. Vol4Ecosse is a non-profit organisation based in Scotland. The group send students to work on community-based projects throughout the country.

   Students can access the Vol4Ecosse website and complete some user forms to update their current location and the status of each project.

   (a) Vol4Ecosse decide to make use of server-side validation when handling forms that keep track of progress.

   Describe **two** reasons why server-side validation may be more appropriate than client-side validation in this case.   **2**

   (b) Whilst volunteering, the students are encouraged to update the status of different projects throughout the country by adding text and photographs to a shared web-based folder. Explain why cloud storage might be best suited for this purpose.   **2**

   (c) The Regulation of Investigatory Powers Act 2000 (RIPA) has implications for Vol4Ecosse and their Internet Service Provider (ISP).

   (i) Describe the financial implications of this Act for ISPs.   **1**

   (ii) Describe **one** reason why RIPA is becoming increasingly difficult to enforce.   **2**

MARKS | DO NOT WRITE IN THIS MARGIN

9. WebScape is a web design company. It is developing a website that will be accessible on many devices including tablets, laptops and smartphones. The site is hosted on their web server.

(a) Describe how accessible design can be achieved using cascading style sheets (CSS).

2

_____

_____

_____

_____

(b) A typical page in the website is tested and requires optimisation.

```
<body>
<script  src="http://webscape.org.uk/js/jquery.js"></script>
<script  src="http://webscape.org.uk/js/jquery.once.js"></script>
<script  src="http://webscape.org.uk/js/drupal.js"></script>
<script  <src="http://webscape.org.uk/js/panels.js"></script>
<style>
.center_div
{
border:1px solid gray;
margin-left:auto;
margin-right:auto;
width:90%;
background-color:#d0f0f6;
text-align:left;
padding:8px;
}
</style>
<img  src="boat1.gif" alt="Big Boat">
<img  src="logo.gif" alt="logo">
<img  src="boat2.gif" alt="Big Boat2">
<img  src="welcome.gif" alt="Welcome Message">
</body>
```

MARKS | DO NOT WRITE IN THIS MARGIN

9. (b) (continued)

   (i)   Explain how the code above could be altered to optimise load times.

2

   (ii) Describe **two** ways that compression can be used to reduce the time to retrieve and display a web page.

2

[END OF SPECIMEN QUESTION PAPER]

ADDITIONAL SPACE FOR ANSWERS

ADDITIONAL SPACE FOR ANSWERS

MARKS | DO NOT WRITE IN THIS MARGIN

HIGHER FOR CfE COMPUTING SCIENCE 34 SQA SPECIMEN PAPER 2014

Model Paper 1

Whilst this Model Paper has been specially commissioned by Hodder Gibson for use as practice for the Higher (for Curriculum for Excellence) exams, the key reference documents remain the SQA Specimen Paper 2014 and SQA Past Paper 2015.

HODDER
GIBSON
LEARN MORE

National
Qualifications
MODEL PAPER 1

Computing Science

Duration — 2 hours

Fill in these boxes and read what is printed below.

Full name of centre

Town

Forename(s)

Surname

Number of seat

Date of birth

Day   Month   Year

D D   M M   Y Y

Scottish candidate number

Total marks — 90

SECTION 1 — 20 marks

Attempt ALL questions.

SECTION 2 — 70 marks

Attempt ALL questions.

Show all workings.

Write your answers clearly in the spaces provided in this booklet. Additional space for answers is provided at the end of this booket. If you use this space you must clearly identify the question number you are attempting.

Use **blue** or **black** ink.

Before leaving the examination room you must give this booklet to the Invigilator; if you do not, you may lose all the marks for this paper.

MARKS | DO NOT WRITE IN THIS MARGIN

SECTION 1 — 20 marks

Attempt ALL questions

1. Artificial intelligence programs may consist of lists of facts and rules that are written in no set order.

   State the type of programming language that is being described.   **1**

2. Describe **one** activity that the passing of the Communications Act in 2003 made illegal.   **1**

3. The following HTML head section is written for a page in a cooking website.

   ```
   <head>
       <link rel="stylesheet" type="text/css" href="recipes.css">
       <title>Chicken Recipes</title>
       <meta name="keywords" content="Cooking">
   </head>
   ```

   (a) The above HTML shows that an external style sheet is being used to format the web page. State **one** advantage gained through using an external style sheet in preference to internal styles.   **1**

   (b) If a user entered "Chicken Recipes" into a search engine this page would not be included in the results. Suggest a solution to this problem.   **2**

4. The memory management function of the operating system ensures that data resident in memory is not overwritten by currently running programs. Describe one other role of the memory management function when opening an additional program.   **1**

MARKS | DO NOT WRITE IN THIS MARGIN

5. A school pupil writes a small computer program to bombard a web server with requests for a particular web page. This has the effect of preventing other users from accessing the website.

   (a) State the law the pupil has broken?   1

   _____

   (b) Explain why bombarding a web server may deny access to legitimate users.   1

   _____

6. Describe how keylogging software poses a security threat to users who are unaware that the program is running on their computer.   2

   _____

   _____

   _____

   _____

7. Explain the role of a trace table when testing a computer program.   2

   _____

   _____

   _____

   _____

MARKS | DO NOT WRITE IN THIS MARGIN

8. The algorithm below is implemented using a procedural programming language.

```
Line 1.  SET total TO 0
Line 2.  SET noOfWeights TO 0
Line 3.  SET weight TO 0
Line 4.  SEND "How many weights do you wish to add up" TO DISPLAY
Line 5.  RECEIVE noOfWeights FROM (INTEGER) KEYBOARD
Line 6.  REPEAT noOfWeights TIMES
Line 7.          SEND "Please enter a weight" TO DISPLAY
Line 8.          RECEIVE weight FROM (REAL) KEYBOARD
Line 9.          SET total TO total + weight
Line 10. END REPEAT
Line 11. SEND "Your total weight is" TO DISPLAY
Line 12. SEND total TO DISPLAY
```

(a) When prompted the user of the program enters the values 4, 3, 7.5, 1.5, 5.

Following this input, state what the output would be from line 12?   1

_____

(b) State the data type that should be declared when initialising the weight variable.   1

_____

9. Open-source programs are increasing in popularity.

State **one** advantage and **one** disadvantage of using open-source programs.   2

_____

_____

_____

_____

MARKS | DO NOT WRITE IN THIS MARGIN

10. A design is drawn showing two subroutines which are called one after the other.

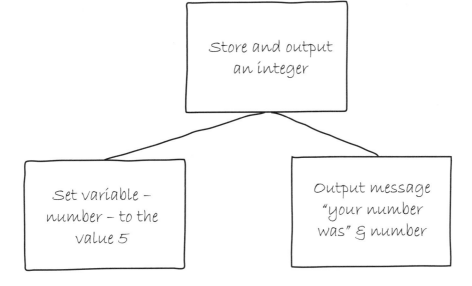

(a) State the design methodology show above.   1

_____

(b) If the design was implemented, without parameter passing and using local variables, what would be the actual output?   2

_____

11. Explain why increasing the amount of cache memory in a computer system improves processing performance.   1

_____

MARKS | DO NOT WRITE IN THIS MARGIN

SECTION 2 — 70 marks

Attempt ALL questions

1. Matthew is designing a program that will store and process information on the calorie content of different biscuits. He uses pseudocode to design how data will be entered into the program.

```
Line 1.   FOR counter FROM 1 TO 10 DO
Line 2.         <get a valid biscuit name>
Line 3.         <get a valid calorie content for the biscuit>
Line 4.   END FOR
```

(a) Explain why the above pseudocode indicates that two arrays will be required when the design is implemented.   1

_____

_____

(b) The calorie content of a biscuit may be an integer ranging from 0 to 200.

   (i) Using pseudocode or a language with which you are familiar, write a refinement of Line 3.   3

   (ii) Describe, using multiple examples of each type of input, how you would comprehensively test your refinement of line 3.   3

_____

_____

_____

_____

MARKS | DO NOT WRITE IN THIS MARGIN

1.   (continued)

(c)   The following function has been used within the program.   The pseudocode for this function is shown below.

```
Line 1.    STRING FUNCTION analysis (biscuitCaloriesArray,
           biscuitNamesArray)
Line 2.    Set maxCalories TO biscuitCaloriesArray[0]
Line 3.    Set maxName TO biscuitNamesArray[0]
Line 4.    FOR counter FROM 1 TO
           Length(biscuitCaloriesArray)
Line 5.        IF biscuitCaloriesArray[counter] >
               maxCalories THEN
Line 6.            SET maxCalories TO
                   biscuitCaloriesArray[counter]
Line 7.            SET maxName TO
                   biscuitNamesArray[counter]
Line 8.        END IF
Line 9.    END FOR
Line 10.   RETURN maxName
Line 11.   END FUNCTION
```

(i)   The two arrays used in lines 2 and 3 are passed as parameters into the function.   State whether the parameters should be passed by value or by reference and explain your answer.   **2**

_____

_____

(ii)   The two arrays hold the following 6 values:

biscuitCaloriesArray	102, 23, 83, 149, 56, 82
biscuitNamesArray	Kit Kat, Rich Tea, Chocolate Digestive, Boasters, Ginger Snaps, Hob Nob

State the output from the function when tested with the above values.   **1**

_____

Total marks   **10**

MARKS | DO NOT WRITE IN THIS MARGIN

2. In 1982, for his 12th birthday, Greg was given a Sinclair ZX Spectrum computer.

The specification of a ZX Spectrum home computer system is shown below.

> Zilog 8 bit processor (16 bit address bus)
>
> 3.5 Mhz clock
>
> 16Kb ROM
>
> 48Kb RAM
>
> 256x192pixel, 4 bit colour output to TV

(a) Like most computers from the 1980s, the ZX Spectrum had no internal backing storage.

  (i) State where the operating system would have been stored?   **1**

  (ii) Describe **one** advantage of storing the operating system in this way.   **1**

MARKS

2. (continued)

(b) The ZX Spectrum had a total of 64 Kb of memory (16 Kb ROM + 48 Kb RAM). Using an appropriate calculation, prove that this was the maximum amount of memory that could have been installed in the computer. **Show your working.**

2

(c) Greg's current computer has a clock speed of 3.5GHz, 1000 times faster than that of the ZX Spectrum. When Greg researches the difference between the raw processing power of his current PC and the Spectrum he finds that his PC is significantly more than 1000 times faster at processing data than the Spectrum.

With reference to differences in computer's architecture (other than clock speed), state two reasons why this is the case.

2

(d) While browsing the world wide web, Greg recently discovered and downloaded a ZX Spectrum emulator which allows him to play all his old games.

Discuss **two** possible hardware issues that the emulator program would have to compensate for when running old spectrum programs on much newer hardware.

2

2.   (continued)

(e)   The ZX Spectrum stored program files on magnetic tape.

A 48Kb game took 5 minutes to load from tape. The sounds were saved in mono at a sampling depth of 1 bit. Calculate the sampling frequency of the sound files used by the Spectrum? **Show your working.**   2

Total marks   10

3. Rory is studying app development at college. As part of a project assignment he creates an app for the members of his local table tennis club. The app will allow its users to store match results, arrange matches with other users and discuss training techniques.

   (a) He uses a graphics package to create a design for the home screen of his app.

   (i) State the type of user Rory is designing the app for. Justify your answer.

2

   _____

   _____

   _____

MARKS

DO NOT WRITE IN THIS MARGIN

3. **(a) (continued)**

    (ii) Describe why the accuracy of the input device being used will be a factor in the design of the user interface.   **1**

_____

_____

    (iii) Describe **one** way the current interface design could be improved.   **1**

_____

_____

(b) During the later stages of development, the table tennis app is Beta tested.

Describe **one** attribute of Beta testing.   **1**

_____

_____

_____

(c) Apps require storage for both program and data files.

    (i) Explain why solid state storage is used in mobile devices.   **1**

_____

    (ii) Briefly describe a current trend in storage systems.   **2**

_____

_____

_____

_____

_____

MARKS

3. (continued)

(d) A later version of the completed app allows users to view current rankings for every user.

(i) Explain why the rankings must be stored remotely from the app.   1

_____

_____

_____

(ii) Describe how this feature could contribute to the growth of online communities.   1

_____

_____

_____

Total marks   9

MARKS | DO NOT WRITE IN THIS MARGIN

4. A computer system collects data from a sensor attached to a wind turbine.

(a) An example reading from the sensor is 302.563 Watts. Each reading is stored in memory as a 32 bit value.

Describe a method that could be used to store a single reading.

2

_____

_____

_____

_____

_____

(b) State the one possible function of the interface required to connect the sensor to the computer.

1

_____

(c) A sub-program is required to read the power being generated once a minute and then calculate the average power reading for each hour. The hourly average is to be stored in a text file. The pseudocode below shows a design for the sub-program.

```
Line 1.  Set averagePower TO 0
Line 2.  Set powerReading TO 0
Line 3.  OPEN FILE "Turbine Readings"
Line 3.  WHILE switch = On
Line 4.      REPEAT 100 TIMES
Line 5.          <wait 60 seconds>
Line 6.          RECEIVE powerReading FROM (REAL) SENSOR
Line 7.          SET averagePower TO averagePower -
                 powerReading
Line 8.      END REPEAT
Line 9.      SET averagePower TO averagePower / 60
Line 10.     RECEIVE averagePower FROM FILE "Turbine
             Readings"
Line 11.     <check if switch is on or off>
Line 12. END WHILE
Line 13. CLOSE FILE "Turbine Readings"
```

MARKS

4. (c) (continued)

The above pseudocode contains three logic errors. Describe each of these errors.　　3

1. _____

_____

2. _____

_____

3. _____

_____

(d) The complete program is implemented using rapid application development techniques. Describe **two** advantages gained by developing the program using this methodology.　　2

_____

_____

_____

_____

(e) The wind farm where the turbine is situated uses a security camera to monitor the site. The camera records compressed video using the following settings: 8 bit colour, 460×320pixel, 2 fps, 50% compression ratio.

Calculate the storage requirements for 1 minute of video. Show your working.　　4

Total marks　12

MARKS | DO NOT WRITE IN THIS MARGIN

5. As a superhero, Catman must keep the manufacture of his crime fighting gadgets a secret.

The gadgets are manufactured as follows.

Each individual component is manufactured by a different company.

A technician employed by Catman's company is given 5 of the components to assemble into a sub unit. A sub unit is only a part of any complete gadget.

Catman himself uses several sub units to assemble each finished gadget.

A relational database with four tables is created to track the manufacture of the each sub unit.

The tables and field names are shown below.

Components	Manufacturers	Sub Unit	Technicians
Component ID	Company ID	Sub Units Name	Forename
Component Name	Company Name	Employee Number*	Surname
Component Price	Address	Component ID*	Gender
Company ID*	Telephone Number	Component ID*	Employee Number
	Bank Account Number	Component ID*	Employee Photo
		Component ID*	Address
		Component ID*	Telephone Number

(a) State a one-to-one relationship that exists between the tables.   1

_____

(b) Explain why the "Sub Units Name" field may be unsuitable as a Primary Key for the Sub Unit Table.   1

(c) Catman uses the following form to enter data for each new technician.

Technician's Detail	
Forename	Jack
Gender	Male
Employee Number	34
Address	99 Alfred Drive Forfar
Telephone Number	01393 638645
Surname	Denton

MARKS | DO NOT WRITE IN THIS MARGIN

5. (c) (continued)

Currently each new data item is typed in by the user. Describe two ways to improve the usability of this form.   **2**

_____

_____

_____

_____

(d) Catman suspects that one of the female technicians has leaked information about one of the sub units. He creates a report detailing all the female technicians that have assembled the "battery pack for grapple hook" sub unit.

Forename	Surname
Sylvia	Trench
Tatiana	Romanova
Jill	Masterton
Domino	Derval
Rosie	Carver

Describe how Catman could use the database software to produce the above list.   **5**

_____

_____

_____

_____

_____

_____

_____

_____

MARKS | DO NOT WRITE IN THIS MARGIN

5. (continued)

(e) The employee photos are stored as png files.

State the **type** of compression used by png and gif files.   1

_____

Total marks   10

MARKS | DO NOT WRITE IN THIS MARGIN

6. Signella manufacture toys for dogs. Their website contains dynamic web pages that display products from their catalogue.

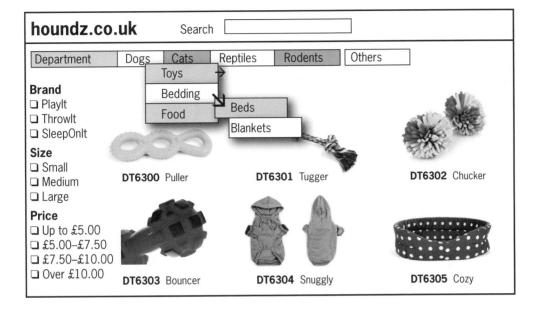

(a) When the customer selects one of the filters shown on the left (for example price between £5 and £7.50) the Signella website uses server-side scripts to extract the required information from a database, create a new page and return the page to the users browser.

   (i) State **two** reasons why generating the web pages using server-side scripts benefits the user of the website.   **2**

_____

_____

_____

_____

_____

_____

   (ii) Name a programming language used in server side scripting.   **1**

_____

(b) As shown in the above image, Signella's website makes use of multi-level navigation.

   Explain how multi-level navigation can aid the accessibility of a website.   **1**

_____

MARKS | DO NOT WRITE IN THIS MARGIN

6. (continued)

(c) Signella's database of products stores a photograph of each toy at a resolution of 1024×768 pixels.

(i) The html tag below is used to display the images of the products on the website.

<img src="ball3.bmp" alt="Bouncy Fetch Ball" width="150" height="100" >

Using information given in the above tag, explain how Signella could optimise the download speed of their web pages.   **2**

_____

_____

_____

(ii) Create a CSS rule that will display a blue border, 1 pixel wide around each the image. The rule should also include a command to create a 20 pixel wide blank area around the image.   **2**

_____

_____

_____

(d) To protect against data loss, Signella back up their database to a second hard disk drive installed within their web server.

Explain why copying data to a second backing storage device within the same computer is not a suitable backup strategy.   **1**

_____

_____

Total marks   10

MARKS | DO NOT WRITE IN THIS MARGIN

7. Smart Applications Ltd are a software company who specialise in creating mobile phone applications for client companies. They have been contracted by Fitboss Gyms to create a mobile phone application that will track the distance its users walk during the course of a day.

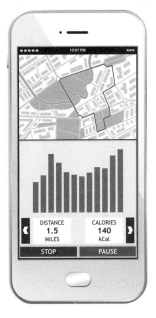

(a) Smart Applications Ltd develop each new mobile phone app for three different mobile operating systems. Explain why multi-platform development may provide their client with a competitive economic advantage.

1

(b) State **three** hardware factors that should be considered when developing applications for mobile devices as opposed to desktop PCs.

3

(c) The distance walked by the user is to be recorded and uploaded to cloud storage every hour.

(i) Other than storing data, describe **two** services that may be provided from cloud storage providers.

2

MARKS | DO NOT WRITE IN THIS MARGIN

7. **(c)** **(continued)**

(ii) State the **type** of cloud storage used by the application.   1

_____

(d) Smart Applications Ltd are asked by their client to ensure that the data created and accessed by the app is secure.

Describe how biometrics and encryption could be used in the app to secure the users data.   2

_____

_____

_____

_____

(e) State why applications have a carbon footprint.   1

_____

_____

Total marks 10

[END OF MODEL PAPER]

MARKS | DO NOT WRITE IN THIS MARGIN

ADDITIONAL SPACE FOR ANSWERS

ADDITIONAL SPACE FOR ANSWERS

Model Paper 2

Whilst this Model Paper has been specially commissioned by Hodder Gibson for use as practice for the Higher (for Curriculum for Excellence) exams, the key reference documents remain the SQA Specimen Paper 2014 and SQA Past Paper 2015.

National
Qualifications
MODEL PAPER 2

Computing Science

Duration — 2 hours

Fill in these boxes and read what is printed below.

Full name of centre

Town

Forename(s)

Surname

Number of seat

Date of birth

Day	Month	Year
D D	M M	Y Y

Scottish candidate number

Total marks — 90

SECTION 1 — 20 marks

Attempt ALL questions.

SECTION 2 — 70 marks

Attempt ALL questions.

Show all workings.

Write your answers clearly in the spaces provided in this booklet. Additional space for answers is provided at the end of this booket. If you use this space you must clearly identify the question number you are attempting.

Use **blue** or **black** ink.

Before leaving the examination room you must give this booklet to the Invigilator; if you do not, you may lose all the marks for this paper.

MARKS | DO NOT WRITE IN THIS MARGIN

SECTION 1 — 20 marks

Attempt ALL questions

1. A stereo ringtone is recorded for a mobile device. The uncompressed sound file is 5 seconds long and was recorded at a sampling rate of 8 Khz with a bit depth of 8 bits.

   Calculate the storage requirements of the ringtone.

   2

2. A long plank of wood is cut into regular lengths.

   Whole plank of wood

   After being cut

   Waste section

   The algorithm below contains two inputs and two possible outputs.

   ```
   Line 1.  RECEIVE lengthOfPlank FROM (REAL) KEYBOARD

   Line 2.  RECEIVE lengthOfCutSections FROM (REAL) KEYBOARD

   Line 3.  IF NOT(MOD(lengthOfPlank/ lengthOfCutSections) = 0) THEN

   Line 4.     SEND [MOD(lengthOfPlank/ lengthOfCutSections) & "
               Left Over"] TO DISPLAY

   Line 5.  ELSE

   Line 6.     SEND "No Waste When Cut" TO DISPLAY

   Line 7.  END IF
   ```

   Using the values 13 and 5 as test data, state and explain the expected output from the algorithm.

   2

MARKS DO NOT WRITE IN THIS MARGIN

3. An object-oriented programming environment uses screen coordinates to move a sprite when the user presses a key on a keyboard.

   A subroutine is designed to move the sprite 10 pixels when the appropriate key is pressed. Part of the design is shown below.

```
Line 1.   PROCUDURE moveSprite (keyPressed, SpriteXCoordinate,
          SpriteYCoordinate)
Line 2.   IF keyPressed = <right cursor key> AND
          SpriteXCoordinate < 240 THEN
Line 3.      SpriteXCoordinate = SpriteXCoordinate + 10
Line 4.   END IF
...
Line 15. END PROCEDURE
```

   (a) When the above design is implemented and tested, by pressing the right cursor key, the sprite does not move. Assuming there are no errors in the code, explain what this tells you about the current x coordinate of the sprite.   1

   (b) State the name given to a subroutine associated with an object in object-oriented programming.   1

4. Explain why saving a program on one computer system and running it on another computer system with an identical specification is not an example of portability.   2

5. A program, written using a high level language, contains an unconditional loop that repeats 1000 times. Explain why a compiled version of the program will run significantly faster than when an interpreter is used to run the high level language code.   1

MARKS | DO NOT WRITE IN THIS MARGIN

6. A string variable is allocated 3200 bits of storage in memory. Assuming Unicode is the format used to store each character calculate the maximum length of the string. **2**

7. Describe **one** advantage of a solid state hard drive over an equivalent magnetic hard disk drive. **1**

8. A program is required to find the first position of a surname in a list. The array used to store the list of surnames is called "competitors".

Using pseudocode or a language of your choice show how the user could enter a surname and how the linear search algorithm could be used to find and display the first position of the entered surname. **4**

MARKS | DO NOT WRITE IN THIS MARGIN

9. The interface below is used to search a database for available holidays.

Please select your preferences

No. of Nights   Country   Vegetarian

1   ○
2   ○ | Egypt | | Yes |
3   ○ | France | | No |
4   ○ | Greece |
5   ◉ | Hawaii |
6   ○ | Japan |
7   ○
>7 ○

(a) Explain why the database form shown above is a good example of a "useable" user interface.

2

_____

_____

_____

(b) Which of the database fields would have the data type Boolean?

1

_____

10. A company uses cloud storage to store its customer database and a database of the products they sell. The customer database is only accessible by the staff and the products database is accessible by both staff and customers. State the type of cloud storage being used.

1

_____

11. Ticketmistress operate a website that sell concert tickets. State why it is important that their hardware is easily scalable.

1

_____

_____

_____

SECTION 2 — 70 marks

Attempt ALL questions

1. A computer program is written to provide Chemistry students with information on simple alcohol molecules. The user will enter the number of carbon atoms in the molecule they wish to look up. The program will use the input to display the three pieces of information shown below.

Possible Inputs by Student	Information Displayed to Student		
Number of Carbon Atoms	Name	Number of Hydrogen Atoms (= Carbon Atoms*2+2)	Chemical Formula of Alcohol (= Carbon Atoms + Hydrogens Atoms + OH)
1	Methanol	4	CH_3OH
2	Ethanol	6	C_2H_5OH
3	Isopropyl alcohol	8	C_3H_7OH

An algorithm is written for the program.

```
Line 1.  <initialise data structure and store required
         information>
Line 2.  <initialise variables>
Line 3.  <ask user to enter a valid number of carbon atoms>
Line 4.  SEND name of alcohol molecule TO DISPLAY
Line 5.  <display the number of hydrogen atoms in the molecule>
Line 6.  <display the chemical formula of the alcohol molecule>
```

(a) The programmer decides that 3 arrays will be required to store the information being displayed to the student.

How would you explain to the programmer that the program does not require as many as 3 arrays?   2

_____

_____

_____

MARKS | DO NOT WRITE IN THIS MARGIN

1. **(continued)**

(b) When entered by the user, the number of carbon atoms is stored in memory as an 8 bit binary number. The method used to store the value is capable of storing positive and negative values.

    (i) Name and describe a method that could be used to store negative binary values.

2

_____

_____

_____

    (ii) State the range of values that your method could store using 8 bits.

2

_____

```
Working
```

    (iii) Explain why it is unnecessary to store negative values in this scenario.

1

_____

_____

(c) The six lines in the algorithm are enclosed with < > symbols to indicate that they should be expanded, giving more detail on how each line should be implemented.

State the name given to the process of expanding each line of the main algorithm enclosed with < > symbols.

1

_____

MARKS | DO NOT WRITE IN THIS MARGIN

1. (continued)

(d) Using pseudocode or a programming language of your choice show how line 5 would be implemented.

2

(e) When the program is implemented, line 3 is written as a subroutine.

(i) State the **type** of parameter passing that would be required when line 3 is implemented.

1

(ii) State the **type** of programming language that is being used if each subroutine is executed one after the other.

1

(f) Explain how a breakpoint could be used to debug the completed program.

2

(g) The functionality of the program is improved at a later date. It now displays information on a variety of other carbon-based molecules as well as alcohols.

State the **type** of maintenance that would have been carried out on the original program.

1

Total marks   15

MARKS | DO NOT WRITE IN THIS MARGIN

2. The diagram below shows a design for a relational database. It shows information about the data being stored and the relationships that exist between the data.

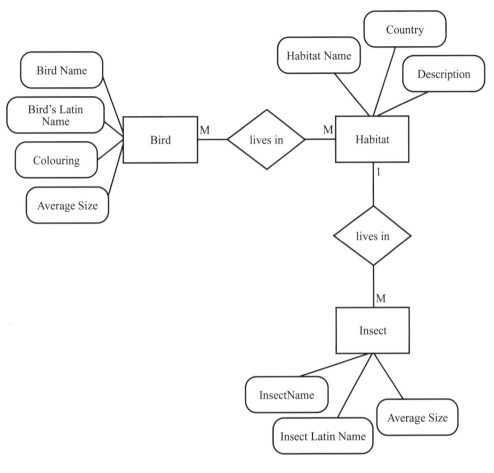

(a) State the **type** of diagram shown above.   1

_____

(b) The diagram indicates that a many-to-many relationship exists between the birds and their habitats.

Explain what this tells us about the relationship between birds and where they live.   2

_____

_____

_____

_____

2. (continued)

(c) Use the diagram to identify one primary key field that should be used when implementing in a database. Name the **one** field and state its data type.

    2

_____

_____

_____

(d) The completed database is hosted on a web server where it can be accessed through a bird watching website.

   (i) Describe how the use of virtual servers benefits companies who are paid to host websites.

    2

_____

_____

_____

_____

   (ii) Describe **two** uses of scripting when a website is linked to a database.

    2

_____

_____

_____

(e) The bird watching website contains a daily blog to which users can add their own comments. Discuss **two** issues relating to censorship and freedom of speech that should be considered when allowing users to add their own comments.

    2

_____

_____

_____

_____

Total marks 11

MARKS | DO NOT WRITE IN THIS MARGIN

3. An electricity supplier maintains a website that allows customers to enter their monthly electricity meter readings. This data is stored and used to produce the customers' annual statements.

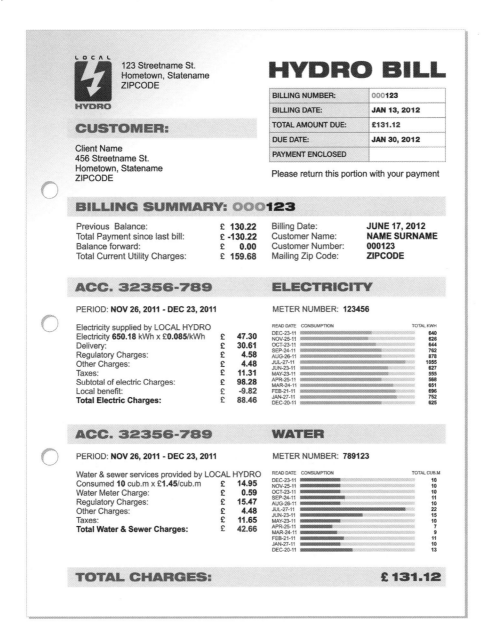

(a) When using the website, customers fill in personal details as shown in the example below.

MARKS | DO NOT WRITE IN THIS MARGIN

3. (a) (continued)

(i) The data in the form is validated using a server-side script. Discuss **one** advantage and **one** disadvantage of server-side validation of form data.

2

_____

_____

_____

_____

(ii) The data in the form contains a variety of different data types. Name a programming data structure suitable for storing the completed form's data on the server and explain precisely how the structure would be organised.

3

_____

_____

_____

_____

(iii) Discuss how you would comprehensively test the inputting of the form data using the script.

4

_____

_____

_____

_____

_____

_____

_____

MARKS | DO NOT WRITE IN THIS MARGIN

3. (continued)

(b) At the end of the year a program reads through all the stored form data to find the final meter reading for the current year. The number of units used is then calculated by subtracting last year's reading. The customer's final bill is the number of units they have used multiplied by the cost of each unit.

An algorithm for the program is shown below.

```
Line 1.  SET customerNumber TO <next customer in database>

Line 2.  SET lastYearsReading TO <customer's previous
         annual meter reading in database>

Line 3.  SET thisYearsReading TO  0

Line 4.  FOR EACH form FROM <all stored forms> DO

Line 5.      IF form.meterReading  < thisYearsReading  AND
             form.customerNumber = customerNumber THEN

Line 6.          SET thisYearsReading TO form.
                 meterReading

Line 7.      END IF

Line 8.  END FOR EACH

Line 9.  SET numberOfUnitsUsed TO thisYearsReading -
         lastYearsReading

Line 10. SET unitPrice TO <value from database>

Line 11. <calculate final cost>

Line 12. <display result as part of a suitable message>
```

(i) Lines 3 to 8 should show an example of the Find Maximum standard algorithm. Identify the logic error in line 5 and explain why the error ensures that the value stored in 'thisYearsReading' at line 9 will always be 0.

2

_____

_____

_____

_____

3. **(b)** **(continued)**

(ii) Line 11 should calculate the final cost for the current year. Line 12 should display the final cost with an appropriate message.

Using pseudocode or a language with which you are familiar show how lines 11 and 12 would be implemented.

3

Total marks   14

MARKS | DO NOT WRITE IN THIS MARGIN

4. Abubakar wishes to learn how to program computer games. His teacher advises him to download and install a programming language at home.

(a) While researching possible languages Abubakar discovers that he could download a variety of proprietary programming languages or open source programming languages.

Stating **one** advantage and **one** disadvantage of each, discuss the differences between the two types of software.   4

(b) Abubakar downloads an open source programming language. While installing the program, Abubakar's security software informs him that the software he is installing contains hidden spyware.

State the purpose of spyware software.   2

(c) After many months Abubakar completes his first computer game and wishes to share it securely with his friend Jill.

Explain the role of Jill's encryption keys when the file is transferred securely.   2

Total marks   8

MARKS | DO NOT WRITE IN THIS MARGIN

5. Interweb Ltd have been hired by a local garden centre to redesign their website. Interweb's design team use wire-framing design notation to create the user-interface shown below.

Banner
(Includes company logo, background photograph, title)

| Home | Plants | Ornaments | Pots | Equipment |

Vegetables
Borders
Shrubs
Tree
Fruit

Scrolling images showing main departments in store and some special offers.

Shopping Basket

Offer of the week

Links to social media
(Facebook, twitter etc)

Footer
(Includes links to: contacts, returns policy, company registration)

(a) Explain why wire-frame diagrams are often referred to as "skeletons". **1**

(b) Explain **two** reasons why wire-framing may save time later when the website is implemented in code. **2**

MARKS | DO NOT WRITE IN THIS MARGIN

5. (continued)

(c) A wire-frame can be used determine the tasks and tools required to build a website.

Identify 2 elements of the wire-frame design that must be implemented using scripts.   **2**

_____

_____

(d) The different areas of the page are created using division, <div>, tags. Explain how a cascading style sheet can be used to apply different styles to each <div> tag.   **1**

_____

_____

(e) The development of the website is broken down into a series of short tasks or iterations which are implemented every two weeks. A small team, who work in the same location, are assigned to each complete iteration.

(i)   State the development methodology being used by Interweb Ltd.   **1**

_____

(ii) Describe **two** advantages to the garden centre of Interweb using this methodology to produce the website.   **2**

_____

_____

_____

_____

MARKS | DO NOT WRITE IN THIS MARGIN

5. (e) (continued)

(iii) One of the principles of good user interface design is consistency. Explain how consistency could be achieved by all the different development teams across multiple pages in a large website.   **3**

_____

_____

_____

_____

_____

_____

_____

_____

Total marks   12

MARKS | DO NOT WRITE IN THIS MARGIN

6. In the last two decades, mobile devices have become part of everyday life. The development of smart phones and tablets were influenced by constant improvement to the internal components of the devices.

(a) One significant change in component technology has been the introduction of multi-core processors.

   (i) Describe how the introduction of multiple cores in mobile devices will influence future software development.   **2**

   (ii) State why a multi-core processor may require a different operating system in order to process data faster than a single-core processor with the same clock speed and bus widths.   **1**

   (iii) Discuss **one** other trend in processor development that may have influenced the success of smart mobile devices in recent years.   **2**

MARKS | DO NOT WRITE IN THIS MARGIN

6.   (continued)

(b) Modern mobile devices regularly inform their users that the operating system may be upgraded.

Explain why updating the operating system often leads to a flurry of available updates for installed applications.

2

_____

_____

_____

_____

(c) Mobile devices regularly connect to networks. Describe three technologies used to connect a mobile device to a network.

3

_____

_____

_____

_____

_____

_____

Total marks   10

[END OF MODEL PAPER]

MARKS | DO NOT WRITE IN THIS MARGIN

ADDITIONAL SPACE FOR ANSWERS

MARKS | DO NOT WRITE IN THIS MARGIN

ADDITIONAL SPACE FOR ANSWERS

Model Paper 3

Whilst this Model Paper has been specially commissioned by Hodder Gibson for use as practice for the Higher (for Curriculum for Excellence) exams, the key reference documents remain the SQA Specimen Paper 2014 and SQA Past Paper 2015.

 HODDER GIBSON
LEARN MORE

National
Qualifications
MODEL PAPER 3

Computing Science

Duration — 2 hours

Fill in these boxes and read what is printed below.

Full name of centre

Town

Forename(s)

Surname

Number of seat

Date of birth
Day   Month   Year

D D   M M   Y Y

Scottish candidate number

Total marks — 90

SECTION 1 — 20 marks

Attempt ALL questions.

SECTION 2 — 70 marks

Attempt ALL questions.

Show all workings.

Write your answers clearly in the spaces provided in this booklet. Additional space for answers is provided at the end of this booket. If you use this space you must clearly identify the question number you are attempting.

Use **blue** or **black** ink.

Before leaving the examination room you must give this booklet to the Invigilator; if you do not, you may lose all the marks for this paper.

MARKS | DO NOT WRITE IN THIS MARGIN

SECTION 1 — 20 marks

Attempt ALL questions

1. Describe **one** way a hacker can cause a denial of service through a DOS attack on a web server.

   1

   _____

   _____

2. Explain why run length encoding is not an appropriate compression technique to apply to a digital photograph with a 32bit colour depth.

   2

   _____

   _____

   _____

   _____

3. Solid state drives are often significantly more expensive than a hard disk drive with an equivalent storage capacity. State **one** reason why a user may still wish to purchase a solid-state drive.

   1

   _____

   _____

4. Look carefully at the pseudocode below

   ```
   SET numberOne TO 5
   SET numberTwo TO 10
   FOR loop FROM 1 TO 3 DO
        SET numberTwo TO numberOne + numberTwo
        SET numberOne TO numberTwo * 2
   END FOR
   ```

   If a program was written using the above design, state what the following variables would store after the program has executed.

   2

   numberOne = _____

   numberTwo = _____

MARKS | DO NOT WRITE IN THIS MARGIN

5. State the **type** of program maintenance required when a mobile phone application is updated following the release of a new operating system for the phone.

1

_____

6. Stating the representation method you use, convert the value -34 into an 8-bit binary number. Show your working.

2

representation method = _____

7. Describe **two** tasks performed by a processor's control unit during a single fetch execute cycle.

2

_____

_____

_____

_____

8. Describe **two** differences between Alpha testing and Beta testing of new software.

2

_____

_____

_____

_____

MARKS | DO NOT WRITE IN THIS MARGIN

9. The software development process is an iterative process.

   (a) Explain why design is regarded as iterative when developing software using rapid application techniques. **1**

   (b) Explain why spending more time during the design phase may reduce the amount of iteration that occurs during the software development process. **2**

10. Some files and applications contain an ID within the data which proves that the file was created by a legitimate source.

    State what is being described above. **1**

11. A company is suspected of the fraudulent selling of fake goods by a Police fraud unit. The Police request that the company help them decrypt e-mails so they can examine communications between the company and their suppliers.

    Explain why it would be a criminal offence for the company to refuse this request. **2**

SECTION 2 — 70 marks

Attempt ALL questions

1. Ross is writing a book to teach beginners how to write computer programs. Before he starts work he purchases a new desktop computer to word process his book. Ross uses a commercial website to order a system with the following specification.

   LabraD quad-core 3.2GHz processor

   2 x 8Gb DDR3 memory modules

   2Tb hard disk drive

   Wireless mouse and keyboard

   2Gb graphics card

   1Gbps network card (wireless enabled)

   Blu-ray Rewriter

   (a) While writing, Ross has the following four applications open, each of which uses the memory resources noted.

SMWord	587Mb
Busy Browser	480Mb
Screenshot Taker	60Mb
DTP Professional	1.8Gb

   (i) If the computer's operating system currently uses 4.2Gb of RAM, calculate the amount of unallocated memory on Ross' computer system.   3

MARKS | DO NOT WRITE IN THIS MARGIN

1. (a) (continued)

    (ii) State the operating system function responsible for ensuring that each of the four applications do not use memory addresses that have already been allocated.

1

_____

  (b) After a week of writing, a virus deletes a file containing the first 10 pages of Ross' book.

    (i) Suggest a backup strategy Ross could implement to reduce the likelihood of further file losses.

2

_____

_____

_____

    (ii) Explain why saving his book to cloud storage could also protect his work from future virus attacks.

1

_____

_____

  (c) A rival author hacks into Ross' computer and copies the unfinished book and deletes the original file. He then publishes parts of the book under his own name.

    (i) With reference to appropriate laws, explain why the rival author has committed two crimes.

4

_____

_____

_____

_____

_____

_____

_____

_____

MARKS | DO NOT WRITE IN THIS MARGIN

1. (c) (continued)

   (ii) Name and describe **two** security precautions Ross could put in place to ensure his work was never stolen again.   2

   _____

   _____

   _____

   _____

   _____

   _____

   (d) State the most significant factor, which determines the data transfer rate when saving a file to cloud storage.   1

   _____

   _____

   Total marks   14

2. Scot Timber Ltd are a large-scale timber company who own 2500 square miles of woodland split in 34 distinct forests. The Scot Timber's forests are each used to grow a single type of tree. Mature trees are cut down and stored in the forests before being sold to customers in a single order. Customers can select the forest from which they buy each of their orders.

(a) A relational database with four tables is created to track the location of each type of wood along with the orders from customers. The tables and field names are shown below.

Wood Types
Wood Name
Wood ID
Years to Mature
Average Trunk Width
Climate
Price Per Tonne

Forest
Wood ID
Forest Name
Location
Public Access

Customers
Customer ID
Customer Name
Address
Account Number
Telephone Number

Order
Order ID
Customer ID
Wood ID
Forest Name
Tonnes Ordered
Total Cost

MARKS | DO NOT WRITE IN THIS MARGIN

2. (a) (continued)

(i) Create a complete entity relationship diagram using the information in the four tables shown on the previous page as entities and state why the diagram shows that this is a poorly designed relational database.

5

(ii) Identify **two** foreign keys and note in which of the four tables the foreign keys are located.

2

(b) The forest table has no primary key. State the type of key that should be created for the forest table and explain your answer.

2

2. (continued)

(c) Explain how the following report could be created.   4

Customer: Bespoke Kitchens Limited				
Order ID	Wood Name	Price per Tonne	Tonnes Ordered	Total Cost
163492	Scots Pine	£552	3	£1656
163493	Mountain Pine	£790	3	£2370
200301	Scots Pine	£554	4	£2216
201020	Oak	£1023	2	£2046

_____

_____

_____

_____

_____

_____

_____

(d) A few of Scot Timber's forests have paths to allow local dog owners to walk their dogs but most are surrounded by fencing to deny public access to the forests.

State the data type that would be used to store the "Public Access" field.   1

_____

(e) Syntax errors are commonly associated with computer programming. Describe a scenario where a syntax error may occur while using a database application.   1

_____

_____

_____

_____

Total marks   15

3. Mighty Racers operate a commercial website to sell remote control cars.

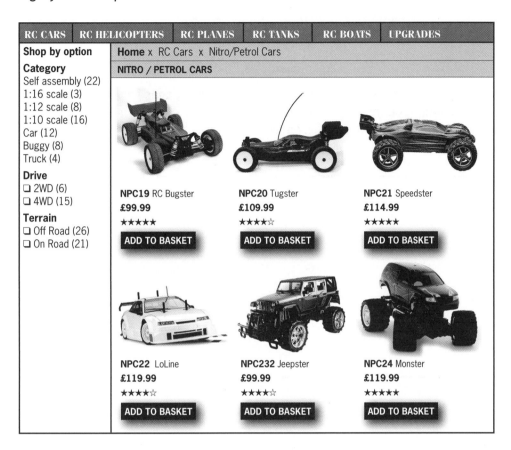

(a) The website uses cascading style sheets to control both the layout and the look of the web pages. An example of a style used throughout the website is shown below.

```
.style1 {
        padding: 2px;
        text-align: center;
        text-transform: capitalize;
        color: white;
        background-color: rgb(255,0,0)
        }
```

(i) Look carefully at the example page from the Mighty Racers website. State the area of the example web page that uses the style shown above and state two reasons for your choice of area.   **3**

_____

_____

_____

_____

_____

_____

MARKS | DO NOT WRITE IN THIS MARGIN

3. (a) (continued)

(ii) State the bit depth of the colour used in "style1".   1

_____

(b) Mighty Racers use an HTML editor to create new web pages for the site. When "new web document" is selected from the editor's menus the following HTML is automatically created. State the purpose of each of the HTML tags shown below.   4

```
<html>
<head>
        <title>Petrol Racers</title>
</head>
<body>
</body>
</html>
```

_____

_____

_____

_____

_____

_____

_____

_____

MARKS

3. (continued)

(c) The Mighty Racers website offers users the option to upload videos of their favourite racing moments. The uploaded videos are converted by a script into mp4 format using lossy, interframe compression techniques.

    (i) Describe how interframe compression reduces the file size of the uploaded videos.

2

    (ii) Explain the difference between lossy and lossless compression.

2

(d) Describe **two** factors that Mighty Racers could consider to ensure that their website is accessible.

2

Total marks   **14**

MARKS | DO NOT WRITE IN THIS MARGIN

4. The diagram below represents a simplified view of the architecture of a computer system CPU and I/O devices.

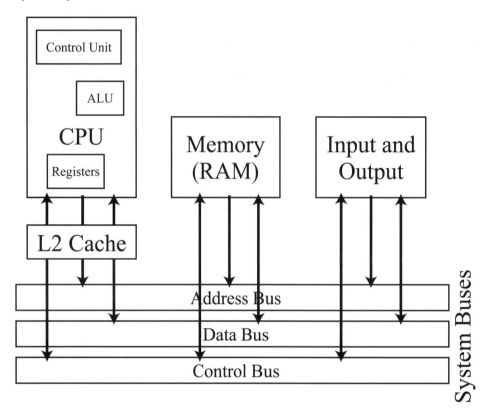

(a) The above diagram shows three different locations where data and instructions may be stored.

Describe how they differ in terms of storage capacity and access time.   **3**

_____

_____

_____

_____

_____

_____

_____

_____

MARKS | DO NOT WRITE IN THIS MARGIN

4. (continued)

(b) The clock speed of a computer system controls the timing of events within the CPU. There has been little increase in clock speeds in the last 10 years.

Describe how other developments in CPU architecture have ensured that processing speeds continue to increase despite the levelling off of clock speeds.

2

_____

_____

_____

_____

_____

_____

_____

(c) Discuss the relationship between the width of the Data and Address Buses and the maximum amount of memory that can be installed on a computer.

3

_____

_____

_____

_____

_____

_____

_____

MARKS | DO NOT WRITE IN THIS MARGIN

4. **(continued)**

(d) The use of electricity throughout the lifetime of a computing component can create a significant carbon footprint.

Describe **two** additional contributing factors that will determine the overall carbon footprint of a computer component during its lifetime.   2

_____

_____

_____

_____

Total marks   10

MARKS | DO NOT WRITE IN THIS MARGIN

5. Jeremy is a keen walker and hill climber. He records the name of the hills he climbs and the height of each hill in a plain text file called "walking diary". The height of each hill is recorded to the nearest foot. A program is being written to analyse the stored data.

The first code to be created reads the data from the text file and stores it in two arrays.

(a) Explain why the programmer stored the values from the text file in two arrays, one of strings and one of integers.   **1**

_____

_____

(b) State an example of an execution error that may occur when a program reads data from a text file.   **1**

_____

_____

(c) Name and describe an alternative data structure that could be used to store the value read from the file.   **2**

_____

_____

_____

_____

(d) Describe the role of the operating system when data is read from a saved file to be stored by a program in a data structure.   **3**

_____

_____

_____

_____

MARKS | DO NOT WRITE IN THIS MARGIN

5. **(continued)**

(e) Reading data from the walking diary file involved the execution of a conditional loop. The loop terminated when there was no more data to read. State the processor component responsible for deciding when the conditions of the loop were met.

1

_____

(f) The two arrays were called hillName and hillHeight. Using pseudocode or a programming language of your choice, design a section of code that will display the name of the highest hill climbed by Jeremy.

6

MARKS | DO NOT WRITE IN THIS MARGIN

5. (continued)

    (g) A Munro is a hill which is at least 3000 feet high. Jeremy wishes to find out how many Munros he has climbed.

        (i) State the standard algorithm which could be used to display the number of Munros Jeremy has climbed.   **1**

        _____

        (ii) The algorithm was written as a function using a procedural programming language. The function finds and displays the number of Munros.

        Would the hillHeight array be passed into the function by value or by reference. Justify your answer.   **2**

        _____

        _____

        _____

        _____

                                                    Total marks   17

                            [END OF MODEL PAPER]

ADDITIONAL SPACE FOR ANSWERS

ADDITIONAL SPACE FOR ANSWERS

MARKS | DO NOT WRITE IN THIS MARGIN

ADDITIONAL SPACE FOR ANSWERS

H

National
Qualifications
2015

Mark

X716/76/01

Computing Science

WEDNESDAY, 6 MAY

9:00 AM – 11:00 AM

Fill in these boxes and read what is printed below.

Full name of centre

Town

Forename(s)

Surname

Number of seat

Date of birth

Day	Month	Year	Scottish candidate number

Total marks — 90

SECTION 1 — 20 marks

Attempt ALL questions.

SECTION 2 — 70 marks

Attempt ALL questions.

Show all working.

Write your answers clearly in the spaces provided in this booklet. Additional space for answers is provided at the end of this booklet. If you use this space you must clearly identify the question number you are attempting.

Use **blue** or **black** ink.

Before leaving the examination room you must give this booklet to the Invigilator; if you do not, you may lose all the marks for this paper.

SQA
©

MARKS | DO NOT WRITE IN THIS MARGIN

SECTION 1 — 20 marks

Attempt ALL questions

1. Convert the decimal number −120 to binary using 8 bits.   **1**

2. Tables can be related by different types of relationships. State the type of relationship between the two tables in each case below.

   (a) People and Hobbies   **1**

   _____

   (b) Jockeys and Horses in a horse race   **1**

   _____

MARKS | DO NOT WRITE IN THIS MARGIN

3. An online company uses a computer program to display particular customer records. The algorithm of this program is shown below.

```
Line 1     SET found TO false
Line 2     RECEIVE search_name FROM (STRING) KEYBOARD
Line 3     FOR counter FROM 0 TO <End Of List> DO
Line 4          IF name[counter] = search_name THEN
Line 5              SET found TO true
Line 6              SEND name[counter] & counter TO DISPLAY
Line 7          END IF
Line 8     END FOR
Line 9     IF found = false THEN
Line 10         SEND "Name not found" TO DISPLAY
Line 11    END IF
```

The following data is stored in the name array:

Jimmy, Samina, Kate, Jimmy, Adam

State the output from the above program if Jimmy is entered at line 2 from the keyboard.

2

4. One feature of a declarative language is the use of facts. Three facts are shown in lines one to three below:

```
Line 1    human(einstein).
Line 2    human(pascal).
Line 3    human(lovelace).

Line 4    mortal(X):-human(X).
```

State the feature being used in line 4 and explain a benefit of its use.

2

[Turn over

MARKS

5. A business is setting up a new communications network. Describe two implications of the Regulation of Investigatory Powers Act (2000) for this business.

2

6. Innes regularly uses a shopping website called Better Shop.

Hello Innes, welcome back and what are you searching for today?

Search

Items recommended to you:

Date: Wednesday 6th May 2015   Time: 21:33

Scripting is used to generate parts of the website.

(a) State **one** part of the website that is generated using client-side scripting.

1

(b) State **one** part of the website that is generated using server-side scripting.

1

MARKS | DO NOT WRITE IN THIS MARGIN

7. Craig has been asked to write an algorithm that will search for a target ID from a list of fifty receipts. Each receipt has a unique receipt ID. Part of the algorithm is shown below.

Line 1	SET found TO false
Line 2	SET counter TO −1
Line 3	RECEIVE target_id FROM (INTEGER) BARCODEREADER
Line 4	REPEAT
Line 5	SET counter TO counter + 1
Line 6	IF receipt_id [counter] = target_id THEN
Line 7	SET found TO true
Line 8	END IF
Line 9	UNTIL _____

Using pseudocode, or a language with which you are familiar, complete line 9 of the algorithm shown above.

2

8. Describe **two** benefits of prototyping when following a rapid application development methodology.

2

_____

_____

_____

_____

9. Explain how cache memory can improve system performance.

2

_____

_____

_____

_____

[Turn over

MARKS | DO NOT WRITE IN THIS MARGIN

10. Describe how usability testing could be carried out on a website.

2

_____

_____

_____

_____

11. A database table may have a compound key. State what is meant by the term compound key.

1

_____

_____

[Turn over for SECTION 2 on *Page eight*]

DO NOT WRITE ON THIS PAGE

MARKS | DO NOT WRITE IN THIS MARGIN

SECTION 2 — 70 marks

Attempt ALL questions

12. A hardware company uses a relational database with the four tables shown below.

Customer	Item	Order	Sale
Customer ID	*Item ID*	*Order no*	Order no *
Customer name	Description	Customer ID *	Item ID *
Customer address	Cost	Date	Quantity
Customer email	Image		

(a) Identify a suitable primary key for the **Sale** table.   1

_____

(b) Draw an *entity-relationship diagram* to illustrate the relationships between the four tables.   3

12. (continued)

(c) A report is produced each time a customer makes an order. An example is shown below.

Customer	Mr D Gryffe	Order no	10728
	12 Gourock Crescent	Date	23/4/15
Item	Number ordered		Cost
Grease spray	1		£6·99
Bell wire (100 m)	1		£8·50
Towel radiator	1		£121·50
Disposable mouse trap	2		£9·98
		Total	£146·97

This report is based on a query. State a list of the tables and fields that would be used in this query and any criteria that would be used to select the above data.

3

_____

_____

_____

_____

_____

_____

(d) The report includes a single total of £146·97 after the four subtotals. Describe how this can be done in the report.

3

_____

_____

_____

_____

_____

_____

MARKS | DO NOT WRITE IN THIS MARGIN

13. EcoCaledonia are an energy company based in Scotland. Sales representatives visit people's houses in an attempt to gain business from new customers.

The sales representatives take a tablet device and often show video clips using apps and mobile websites.

(a) Describe how quad-core processors can be used to improve load times for web apps containing client-side scripts or multimedia.   **2**

_____

_____

_____

_____

(b) Describe how compression reduces the file size of videos.   **3**

_____

_____

_____

_____

_____

_____

MARKS | DO NOT WRITE IN THIS MARGIN

13. (continued)

(c) EcoCaledonia plan to launch an app that will allow customers with Internet access to turn their heating system on using a mobile device.

Describe how EcoCaledonia could ensure that all customers could use the software regardless of the operating system on their device.

2

_____

_____

_____

_____

(d) Customers of EcoCaledonia can sign in to their account to supply meter readings, pay bills and update contact details.

Explain how their details are secure when transmitted.

3

_____

_____

_____

_____

_____

_____

[Turn over

MARKS | DO NOT WRITE IN THIS MARGIN

13.   (continued)

(e)   When signing in to their account customers have to enter details from their username and password as shown below.

```
┌──────────────────────────────────────────┐
│  ┌────────────────────────────────────┐  │
│  │ Your username                      │  │
│  │ Enter the following characters     │  │
│  │ from your username                 │  │
│  │                                    │  │
│  │ Enter the 3rd character    [ • ]   │  │
│  │                                    │  │
│  │ Enter the 4th character    [ • ]   │  │
│  │                                    │  │
│  │ Enter the 1st character    [ • ]   │  │
│  │                                    │  │
│  │ Your password                      │  │
│  │ Enter the following characters     │  │
│  │ from your password                 │  │
│  │                                    │  │
│  │ Enter the 3rd character    [ • ]   │  │
│  │                                    │  │
│  │ Enter the 4th character    [ • ]   │  │
│  │                                    │  │
│  │ Enter the 1st character    [ • ]   │  │
│  │                                    │  │
│  │            ⬅   ➡                    │  │
│  └────────────────────────────────────┘  │
└──────────────────────────────────────────┘
```

Explain why customers are asked to enter their details in a random order each time.   1

_____

_____

[Turn over for Question 14 on *Page fourteen*]

DO NOT WRITE ON THIS PAGE

MARKS DO NOT WRITE IN THIS MARGIN

14. EcoCaledonia recruits employees using an online application form. Rowena completes her form and receives the feedback below:

Please correct the following information

* Indicates required fields

Title: *   Miss ⌄

First name: *   Rowena

Surname: *   Drayton

Gender: *   ○ Male ◉ Female

Email address: *   rowenadrayton@schoolmail.co.uk

Mobile phone number: 077g6367324

Please enter a valid mobile phone number

Are you happy to receive information from our partner companies   ☑

(a) State the most appropriate data type used to store the value of the "receive information" check box.   1

_____

(b) Rowena accidentally entered an invalid mobile phone number and an error message is displayed. A valid mobile phone number will consist of a string of 11 digits.

Using pseudocode or a programming language of your choice, write the algorithm which would check that the mobile phone number is valid.   5

MARKS | DO NOT WRITE IN THIS MARGIN

14. (continued)

(c) An algorithm is implemented to validate the applicant's data from the application form opposite. There are two subprograms at lines two and three. The parameters for these subprograms are not shown.

```
Line 1      REPEAT
Line 2          Enter_applicant_data (…)
Line 3          Validate_form_data (…)
Line 4      UNTIL <form data is valid>
```

Name a parameter that should be passed at line 2, state the type of parameter passing used and justify your answer.   2

_____

_____

_____

_____

(d) EcoCaledonia has its own servers which need to be upgraded and is considering migrating to a hybrid cloud.

(i) Describe what is meant by a hybrid cloud.   1

_____

_____

(ii) State **two** advantages for EcoCaledonia of switching to a hybrid cloud.   2

_____

_____

_____

_____

[Turn over

MARKS | DO NOT WRITE IN THIS MARGIN

15. A local hair salon has a desktop computer, a tablet computer and a printer. These devices are networked using a wireless connection.

(a) The hair salon needs to use software that is only available for an older operating system. State how the hair salon could run this software on their system.

1

_____

_____

(b) Staff can access all files on the network. Customers can only access a catalogue file of various hair styles. Describe how the operating system allows these restrictions to be set up.

2

_____

_____

_____

_____

(c) A digital camera is used to take the customer's photograph and then the camera is connected to the desktop computer using an interface.

(i) State **two** tasks undertaken by an interface when transferring these photographs to the desktop computer.

2

_____

_____

_____

_____

(ii) The photograph can then be edited so that the customer can view it with a range of hair styles and colours. This photograph could be a bitmap or vector graphic. Select one type of graphic and explain why it is suitable for this purpose.

2

_____

_____

_____

_____

MARKS | DO NOT WRITE IN THIS MARGIN

15. (continued)

(d) The hair salon also has some video clips stored on their computer that they use to train staff.

Calculate the uncompressed file size of one of these video clips which is 90 seconds long and was captured at 25 frames per second with a resolution of 260 by 200 pixels and 16 777 216 colours.

State your answer in appropriate units and show all working.   **2**

(e) The manager of the hair salon is considering whether to buy new computers or to upgrade the existing ones.

(i) Describe **one** environmental advantage of upgrading.   **1**

_____

_____

(ii) Describe **one** environmental advantage of buying new computers.   **1**

_____

_____

[Turn over

MARKS | DO NOT WRITE IN THIS MARGIN

16. Joseph has been asked to develop a website for the Glasburgh Safari Park where visitors can go to see animals including pandas. Joseph often makes use of cascading style sheets which can be internal or external.

(a) Describe the difference between an internal style sheet and an external style sheet.

2

_____

_____

_____

_____

(b) Explain why the use of external style sheets may result in optimal load times when compared to the use of internal style sheets.

2

_____

_____

_____

_____

(c) Joseph is using an external style sheet named "masterstyle". Complete the HTML code that will successfully link to this stylesheet.

2

<link rel = _____ type= "text/css" href= _____>

(d) Joseph includes a rule in the external style sheet to make all the large headings appear in Tahoma font, blue and centred wherever they appear on each page.

Write a CSS rule to manage these large headings.

3

MARKS | DO NOT WRITE IN THIS MARGIN

16. (continued)

(e) Searching for the 'Glasburgh Safari' or 'pandas' on the World Wide Web with a search engine does not give a prominent result for this site. Describe **two** ways that Joseph can improve this without incurring any further costs.

2

_____

_____

_____

_____

(f) Customers can purchase tickets via the website.

Explain how the use of a database driven website would allow the safari park to display a message if there were only a small number of tickets left on a certain day.

2

_____

_____

_____

_____

[Turn over

MARKS | DO NOT WRITE IN THIS MARGIN

17. Chris wants a program to process information about each of the pupils in his class.

Line 1	RECORD Test_marks IS {STRING surname, INTEGER mark_1, INTEGER mark_2, INTEGER mark_3, STRING email}
Line 2	SET pupil[1] TO ("Smith", 67, 89, 91, "john@doodle.co.uk")
Line 3	SET pupil[2] TO ("Latif", 42, 91, 84, "fatima@doodle.co.uk")
Line 4	SEND pupil[1].mark_2 TO DISPLAY

(a) (i) Explain the purpose of line 2.   2

_____

_____

_____

_____

(ii) State the output from line 4.   1

_____

_____

(iii) Chris wants to calculate the average for the first pupil. Using pseudocode, or a language with which you are familiar, write the line to calculate this average.   2

MARKS | DO NOT WRITE IN THIS MARGIN

17. (continued)

(b) Chris calculates the average mark for each pupil and stores the average marks in an array. He writes the following pseudocode to count the number of grade A passes of 70 or more:

```
Line 1    SET list TO [74.33, 57.67, 73.33, 82.33]
Line 2    SET amount TO 0
Line 3    FOR counter FROM 0 TO 2 DO
Line 4        IF list[counter] >= 70 THEN
Line 5            SET amount TO amount + 1
Line 6        END IF
Line 7    END FOR
Line 8    SEND amount TO DISPLAY
```

When Chris tests the program, it outputs the wrong number of A passes.

(i) State the output from the code above.   1

(ii) State the name of this type of error.   1

(iii) Identify and correct the line of the algorithm which contains the error.   2

[Turn over for Question 17(c) on *Page twenty-two*

MARKS | DO NOT WRITE IN THIS MARGIN

17. **(continued)**

(c) Chris creates an algorithm that will search the array of average marks and return the smallest value present.

```
Line 1 SET list to [74.33, 57.67, 73.33, 87.33]
Line 2 SET minimum TO list [0]
Line 3 FOR counter FROM 1 TO 3 DO
Line 4     IF minimum > list[counter] THEN
Line 5          SET minimum TO list[counter]
Line 6     END IF
Line 7 END FOR
```

A trace table is used to record the change to a variable at the corresponding line number. Part of the trace table is shown below. State the values missing from the trace table below at A, B and C.

Line	list	minimum	counter
1	74.33, 57.67, 73.33, 87.33		
2		A	
3			B
5		C	
3	....	....	....

3

A _____

B _____

C _____

(d) Explain how breakpoints could be used in conjunction with a trace table to locate errors in code.

2

_____

_____

_____

_____

[END OF QUESTION PAPER]

ADDITIONAL SPACE FOR ANSWERS

MARKS | DO NOT WRITE IN THIS MARGIN

ADDITIONAL SPACE FOR ANSWERS

SQA AND HODDER GIBSON HIGHER FOR CfE COMPUTING SCIENCE 2015

Section 1

Question		Expected Answer(s)	Max mark
1.	(a)	Last stage of testing prior to release.	1
	(b)	*Any two of the following:* • software can be tested on their own systems • software can be tested on eventual users • provide feedback to software development company • client needs to agree that software meets their needs before accepting/ paying for it	2
2.		Line 6: found = true (1 mark). Line 9: UNTIL found = true or counter = 101 (1 mark).	2
3.		To run the object code/exe/machine code (1 mark) for a different processor than the one in the computer (1 mark).	2
4.		Incremental backups (1 mark) would ensure no loss of transaction data in between the daily backups (1 mark).	2
5.	(a)	RAD involves the creation of prototypes/models/working software. Prototypes can stimulate user interest in the software as they can use/see a working copy with limited features.	2
	(b)	*Any two of the following:* • regular opportunities to assess development/success • shorter iterations of work/quicker response to change • gather requirements at the same time as developing software • greater customer collaboration/ cooperation	2
6.		Allocates 16 bits for the exponent (1 mark) and 16 bits for mantissa (1 mark). Two's complement for the mantissa would allow negative values (1 mark). **OR** Two's complement for the exponent to allow for small values (1 mark).	3

Question		Expected Answer(s)	Max mark
7.	(a)	Compiler saves the object code (1 mark) and so does not retranslate on each pass through the loop (1 mark). **OR** Interpreter may retranslate (1 mark) on each pass through the loop using processor time (1 mark). **OR** Interpreter resident in memory (1 mark), compiler doesn't need to be in memory (1 mark).	2
	(b)	Faster access time (1 mark) than main memory (1 mark). **OR** Entire section of code will be present in cache (1 mark), and so cache misses will not occur (1 mark).	2

Section 2

Question			Expected Answer(s)	Max mark
1.	(a)		*Any two of the following:* • only one line of code required to create multiple values • can be traversed using loop structure • parameter passing easily implemented with one line • efficiency of code • each individual element in the array can be referenced by indexing	2
	(b)	(i)	(see table below)	3
		(ii)	Counter goes back to 1 on every iteration of the loop (1 mark), causing the terminating condition of the loop never to be met (1 mark).	2
		(iii)	Change line 5 (1 mark) to SET position TO counter (1 mark).	2
		(iv)	A logic error where the program produces incorrect or undesired output (1 mark), possibly as the result of an incorrect formula or using an incorrect or wrong algorithm (1 mark).	2
	(c)		The use of breakpoints (1 mark) allows execution of code to be stopped at a pre-defined point (1 mark).	2

Table for Question 1 (b) (i):

Line	Source	Position	Counter
1	[77,66,88,67,89,72]		
2		1	
3			2
5			1

Question			Expected Answer(s)	Max mark
2.	(a)		The value of salary will be 60000; none of the IF statement conditions becomes true as 60000 is not less than or greater than 60000, so the variable taxcode will remain at "Z".	2

	(b)		SET taxcode TO "Z"
			
			SET salary TO (income1 + income2)
			
			IF salary < 9000 THEN
			  SET taxcode to "A"
			
			ELSE IF salary >= 9000 AND salary < 43000 THEN
			  SET taxcode to "B"
			
			ELSE IF salary >= 43000 AND salary < 60000 THEN
			  SET taxcode to "C"
			
			ELSE IF salary >= 60000 THEN
			  SET taxcode to "D"
			
			END IF
			
			RETURN taxcode
			
			SET taxcode TO "Z"
			
			SET salary TO (income1 + income2)
			
			SELECT CASE salary
			  CASE < 9000: SET taxcode to "A"
			  CASE 9000 to 43000: SET taxcode to "B"
			  CASE > 43000 AND < 6000: SET taxcode to "C"
			  CASE >= 60000: SET taxcode to "D"
			END SELECT
			RETURN taxcode
				3

	(c)		RECEIVE salary FROM KEYBOARD RECEIVE bonus FROM KEYBOARD code = taxcode (salary, bonus) SEND code TO DISPLAY	3
	(d)		Navigational structure – relationship between links and take account of the nature of navigation (1 mark). Accept examples of nature, eg local navigation to a page/global links to other parts of system. Presentation of data – placement of objects to maximise purpose of page for end user, eg priority of visual elements like a file player/image/legal information (1 mark). Interface design – matches hardware used to communicate with page or takes account of ease of use, eg check boxes instead of text boxes.	2

Question			Expected Answer(s)	Max mark

3.	(a)		SET frequency TO 0
			FOR counter FROM 1 TO 30
			  IF rainfall[counter]=0 AND lowtemp[counter]<0 THEN
			    SET frequency TO frequency+1
			  END IF
			END FOR
			OPEN drydays
			  SEND frequency TO drydays
			CLOSE drydays
				5

	(b)		By declaring it as a parameter which can pass a value to a corresponding parameter (1 mark).	1
4.	(a)		*Any two of the following:* • dynamic web pages will respond to information entered by the visitor • information will always be recent/up to date • visitors will be presented with information that relates specifically to their needs	2

	(b)		H3 {
			`font-family : Tahoma;`
			`font-size : 16px;`
			`color : red;`
			`font-weight : bold`
			    }
			Acceptable alternatives to H3:
			.subheading { rules }
			OR
			#subheading1 {rules}
				3

	(c)		• the username should be validated against the list of existing usernames • when registering, the system must ensure that the username does not already exist in the database • to check that no invalid characters are included	1
	(d)		atpos(8)<2 is false; dotpos(3)<atpos+2(10) is true dotpos+2 (5)>=length(11) is false as one condition is true, the expression is true, so alert message is displayed	3
5.	(a)		Candidate might describe an autonomous robotic device, or a game-playing program that can learn and develop strategies, or a system that replicates human conversation. Examples could be in commercial use, or at a research stage, or games-based. Note that the description should be of a contemporary development, so reference to historical programs like Eliza would not be appropriate.	2
	(b)		Example must clearly show an economic benefit resulting from the system described.	1

Question		Expected Answer(s)	Max mark
	(c)	Example must clearly show a problem for society resulting from the system described.	1
6.	(a)	*Any two of the following:* • walker and walk • dog and walk • owner and dog	2
	(b)	• make the gender/walks well with others options Boolean with a male/female and yes/no buttons • create drop down lists for Dog type and Owner ID	2
	(c)	Create a query with the following fields: • Walker.walker name and criteria = "Susan" • Dog.dogname • Dog.dogtype • Dog.walks well with others • Owner.owner address And then create a report using the data from the query.	5
7.	(a)	*Any two of the following:* • ensure that the title tag contains a concise description of the website's content • create a new title tag for each web page • use the description meta tag to add more detail about the page • use URLs that are as concise as possible • do not use generic titles for URLs, page titles or meta data, eg page1, etc • create an XML sitemap for submission to the software company managing the crawler Or any other valid response.	2
	(b)	They could have used more appropriate alt tags (1 mark), to include a better description of each image (1 mark).	2
	(c)	It has long runs of pixels of the same colour(1 mark), allowing the colour and the repetitions to be stored using just two values (1 mark).	2
8.	(a)	*Any two of the following:* • updating centrally held data/data sources is not possible with client side scripting • validation cannot be disabled if it is handled at the server • can query SQL using PHP • less security issues as data is managed at server Or any other valid response.	2

Question			Expected Answer(s)	Max mark
	(b)		*Any two of the following:* • allows multiple uses to share, edit and save files/folders • accessible via the internet from any device • accessible via internet from any location	2
	(c)	(i)	ISPs must implement technical systems for the storing and interception of information that may be requested by government.	1
		(ii)	Encryption is becoming more sophisticated/difficult to decrypt, etc (1 mark), requiring the cooperation of the individual to provide keys/information in order to decrypt (1 mark).	2
9.	(a)		CSS media queries are used to identify the target device/screen (1 mark). CSS rules are created for different devices/screen widths (1 mark). *1 mark for each correct response.*	2
	(b)	(i)	*Any one of the following:* • Create a CSS file to hold the CSS rules so that less data is delivered with main page. • Merge the JavaScript files into one and include file to reduce fetches from the server. • Merge the images into one image and use CSS rules to display only the relevant area of the image. This reduces the number of fetches from server.	2
		(ii)	• Compression is used when the page is served, thus reducing the amount of data sent to the browser. The browser will decompress the page data when received. **OR** • Compression reduces the amount of data exchanged from the server to the browser client, therefore reducing the time taken to load the data.	2

HIGHER FOR CfE COMPUTING SCIENCE MODEL PAPER 1

Section 1

Question			Expected Answer(s)	Max mark
1.			Declarative	1
2.			*One mark for any one of the following:* • dishonestly obtaining electronic communications services • possession of equipment used to dishonestly obtain communications services • improper use of a public electronic communications network • an example of the above (for example – SIM card cloning, trolling)	1
3.	(a)		The styles in an external style sheet can be applied to multiple pages.	1
	(b)		The words "Chicken" and "Recipes" (1 mark) should be added to the meta tag (1 mark).	2
4.			Memory management allocates sufficient memory address for the additional application.	1
5.	(a)		Computer Misuse Act	1
	(b)		Bombardment may cause resource starvation.	1
6.			Keylogging software stores every character entered on a keyboard which may include usernames and passwords (1 mark). The captured data may be used by another user to gain access to protected information or websites (such as online backing) (1 mark).	2
7.			A trace table records how a variable changes value when code is executed (1 mark). This helps the programmer find where errors are occurring (1 mark).	2
8.	(a)		17 (loop 4 times then add 3 + 7.5 + 1.5 + 5)	1
	(b)		real	1
9.			**Advantages:** *(1 mark for any one of the following)* • it's usually free • it can be adapted to your specific needs • it evolves in response to the needs of the community using the software **Disadvantages:** *(1 mark for any one of the following)* • user interface often poorer • might be less support available if problems • although free there may be hidden costs such as additional support • as anyone in the community may adapt the software it is more open to abuse such as virus insertion	2
10.	(a)		Structure Diagram	1
	(b)		your number was 0 (text – 1 mark, value – 1 mark).	2

Question			Expected Answer(s)	Max mark
11.			Cache memory can store an increased number of frequently used instructions reducing the number of times instructions are read from the slower main memory.	1

Section 2

Question			Expected Answer(s)	Max mark
1.	(a)		The pseudocode shows two inputs inside a loop which tells us that the two inputs must be stored multiple times before the values are then used elsewhere in the program.	1

	(b)	(i)	REPEAT
			    RECEIVE calorieContent FROM (INTEGER) KEYBOARD (1 mark)
			    IF calorieContent < 0 OR calorieContent >200 SEND "Error message" TO DISPLAY (1 mark)
			UNTIL calorieContent>=0 AND calorieContent<=200 (1 mark)
			OR
			RECEIVE calorieContent FROM (INTEGER) KEYBOARD (1 mark for both RECEIVE lines)
			WHILE calorieContent<0 OR calorieContent>200 (1 mark)
			    SEND "Error message" TO DISPLAY (1 mark)
			    RECEIVE calorieContent FROM (INTEGER) KEYBOARD
			REPEAT
				3

		(ii)	To comprehensively test a program, test data should include: Normal test data – 12, 199, 54 etc (1 mark for two examples between 0 and 200) Extreme test data – 0 and 200 (1 mark for both) Exceptional test data – 345, -42, etc (1 mark for two examples outwith 0 and 200)	3
	(c)	(i)	Passed by Value (1 mark). Data is passed in but is not altered (1 mark).	2
		(ii)	Boasters	1
2.	(a)	(i)	The operating system would be stored in ROM.	1
		(ii)	The contents can't be changed/deleted (1 mark). **OR** no loading required/accessed instantly (1 mark).	1

Question			Expected Answer(s)	Max mark
	(b)		Maximum Installable Memory = $2^{\text{address bus width}}$ * data bus width Maximum Installable Memory = 2^{16} * 1 byte (1 mark) Maximum Installable Memory = 65,536 bytes Maximum Installable Memory = 64Kb (1 mark)	2
	(c)		*Any two from the following:* • The newer PC will have wider buses allowing for greater throughput of data • The newer PC may have a multi-core processor • The newer PC may have cache memory • The newer PC's processor will have an increased number of internal registers	2
	(d)		*Any two from the following:* • The emulator will have to ensure that the games' instructions are processed at the same speed of the original hardware • The emulator will have to compensate for the differences in the colour depth of the game's graphics and a modern high-colour monitor when displaying the old game • The emulator will have to compensate for the differences in low resolution of the game's graphics and a modern high-colour monitor when displaying the old game • The emulator will have to allow for the use of modern input devices (mouse) that did not exist when to older computer was in use	2
	(e)		Use the formula for working out the size of a sound file, reorder the equation to calculate the sampling frequency. sampling frequency * sampling depth * channels * length (secs) = size of file sampling frequency * 1bit * 1 * (5*60) secs = 48Kb (1 mark) sampling frequency = (48*1024*8 bits) / (1bit*1*300secs) (1 mark) sampling frequency = 393216 bits / 300bits per sec sampling frequency = 1310.72 Hz	2
3.	(a)	(i)	The app is being designed for novice users as it has a simple, easy-to-use layout.	1

Question			Expected Answer(s)	Max mark
		(ii)	*Any one from the following:* • If an object is too small, the accuracy of the touchscreen may make it difficult to select the object • The accuracy of the touchscreen will determine the minimum size of screen objects	1
		(iii)	*Any one from the following:* • Proper names could be given to the menus instead of single letters • The icons on the menu screen could be increased in size • Contrasting colours could be used to make the objects stand out more	1
	(b)		*Any one from the following:* • Beta testing may be undertaken by persons outwith the programming team • Beta testing will involve use of a complete (but not bug-free) product • Beta testing will test how software runs on hardware other than the hardware the software was written on	1
	(c)	(i)	Low power consumption preserves battery life or small physical size fits easily inside small portable devices.	1
		(ii)	*Any two from:* • Storage devices are reducing in size • More data can be stored in an increasingly smaller physical space • The cost per unit of storage is continually reducing • New storage devices may have reduced power requirements	2
	(d)	(i)	Each user has their own rank. To share this with every other user, central storage is required.	
		(ii)	Rory's app would allow a means to learn more about table tennis players encouraging the growth of the online community.	1
4.	(a)		The number would be stored as two values, a mantissa and an exponent (1 mark) with a section of the 32bits being allocated to each value (1 mark). Note 1 – If the answer given suggests that 2 *32 bits (double precision) is used, this should be accepted. Note 2 – this answer could also be written as an example. 24 of the 32 bits could be used to store the mantissa with the remaining 8 bits being allocated to the storage of the exponent.	2
	(b)		*Any two from the following:* • Voltage conversion • Analogue to Digital Conversion • Compensating for differences in data transfer rates • Data format conversion	1

Question		Expected Answer(s)	Max mark
(c)		*1 mark for each correctly identified error below:* Error 1 – Line 4, should read REPEAT 60 TIMES (1 repeat for each minute in the hour) Error 2 – Line 7, last part should add powerReading on to averagePower and not subtract it Error 3 – Line 10, the averagePower should be written to the file and not read from it	3
(d)		*Any two from the following:* • Development teams can respond quickly to changing customer requirements • Continual contact with customer ensures that the development team are not guessing the wishes of the client • Testing is completed as the project progresses so errors are found earlier • Projects are often more enjoyable as regular goals are reached • Software is produced faster giving economic benefits to client and developer	2
(e)		Use the formula below to calculate the uncompressed size of a video file. Uncompressed video file size = resolution * colour depth * frames per second * length of video (seconds) Uncompressed video file size = 460*320 * 8bits * 2fps * 60seconds (1 mark for first three values, 1 mark for time) Uncompressed video file size = 141,312,000bits Uncompressed video file size = 16.846Mb (1 mark) The file has been compressed by 50% so is therefore half the size of the original uncompressed file = 8.423Mb (1 mark).	4
5. (a)		*Any one from the following:* • Components Table to Manufacturers Table (one component is manufactured by one manufacturer)	1
(b)		A Primary Key should be a unique value. It may be possible the two sub units have the same name making this field unsuitable as a Primary Key field.	1

Question		Expected Answer(s)	Max mark
(c)		*Any two from the following:* • The Gender field should have a restricted choice (drop down menu or radio button) to speed up entry of data and reduce errors • The Employee Number field should be generated automatically instead of requiring the user to enter it • The Surname field should follow the Forename field as data is entered faster by a user when it is in a logical order • Length checks could be used to inform the user when they have entered invalid data, for example the telephone number	2
(d)		Create a query (1 mark) with the following fields: Sub Unit Table.Sub Units Name and criteria = "battery pack for grapple hook" (1 mark). Technicians Table.Forname (1 mark). Technicians Table.Surname (1 mark). Create a report using the Forname and Surname fields from the query (1 mark).	5
(e)		Lossless compression	1
6. (a)	(i)	*Any two from the following:* • Load times of web pages generated server side are generally faster • The interactivity of the website will be improved allowing the website to respond to the users actions (show related items etc) • The user does not require additional plugins or browser scripting technology to view the website	2
	(ii)	*Any one from the following list of programming languages:* ASP, ANSI C scripts, ColdFusion Markup Language, Java, JavaScript (using Server-side JavaScript), PHP, SMX, Lasso, WebDNA, Progress® WebSpeed®.	1
(b)		Multi-level navigation reduces clutter on the page making links easier to find. (1 mark). Multi-level navigation reduces the need to navigate through multiple web pages to find the correct page (1 mark).	1

Question			Expected Answer(s)	Max mark
	(c)	(i)	The original images should be edited to reduce the resolution to that used on the webpage (i.e. from 1024x768 to 150x100) (1 mark). The graphics are currently uncompressed bmp files. They should be converted to a file type that allows compression (1 mark). Revision note – both of these techniques reduce the amount of data being transferred which reduces the load times of each web page.	2
		(ii)	.imageformat { border-width : 1px; (1 mark) border-color : blue; (1 mark) padding : 20px (1 mark) }	3
	(d)		A second backup disk within the same computer system is vulnerable to the same risks that may damage the first disk (for example, virus infection, fire, high magnetic field etc).	1
7.	(a)		Programs available for multiple platforms will have increased sales.	1
	(b)		*Any three from the following:* • Reduced processing capability of mobile devices • Limited backing storage • Limited memory • Touchscreen input (as opposed to keyboard and mouse) • Screen can be rotated between landscape and portrait	3
	(c)	(i)	*Any two from the following:* • Encryption of files • Different payment methods • Peer to peer network setup • Public file hosting • Choice of where data is located (which country) • Cloud hosted Net Drive • Automatic backup of data	2
		(ii)	Public Cloud Storage	1
	(d)		Biometric such as Voice Recognition or Fingerprint Recognition could be used to ensure only the user accesses the data. Encryption could be used to make the data unreadable should it be accessed without permission.	2
	(e)		The creation and use of an application requires a running computer that uses electricity. The production of electricity always has a carbon footprint.	1

HIGHER FOR CfE COMPUTING SCIENCE MODEL PAPER 2

Section 1

Question			Expected Answer(s)	Max mark
1.			size of sound file = sampling frequency * sampling depth * channels * length (secs) size of sound file = 8000 Hz * 8 bits * 2 * 5 secs (1 mark) size of sound file = 640,000 bits size of sound file = 78.125 Kb	2
2.			1 mark for output '3 Left Over' 1 mark for explaining that the first output is displayed as the modulus function calculates that the remainder of 13/5 is not 0.	2
3.	(a)		The x coordinate is already greater than or equal to 240.	1
	(b)		Method	1
4.			A program is only portable it is runs under different conditions (1 mark) therefore moving a program to a computer with the same hardware and operating system is not an example of portability (1 mark).	2
5.			The interpreter will translate and execute the code within the loop 1000 times causing the program to run significantly slower than an executable program translated once by a compiler.	1
6.			In Unicode one character = 16 bits (1 mark). 3200/16 = 200 characters (1 mark).	2
7.			*Any one from the following:* • More robust as no moving parts • Faster read/write speed to flash memory	1

Question		Expected Answer(s)	Max mark

8.		The answer below is given in pseudocode. For an answer written in a programming language, match the answers below to the appropriate line of code.
		
		SEND "Enter the surname you wish to find" TO DISPLAY
		
		RECEIVE surname FROM (STRING) KEYBOARD
		
		SET counter TO 0
		(1 mark for initialising variables)
		
		SET found TO False
		
		REPEAT
		
		   IF competitors[counter] = surname THEN (1 mark for IF conditions and output below)
		
		   SEND ["The first instance of" & surname & "was at position" & counter] TO DISPLAY
		
		   SET found TO True
		
		   END IF
		
		   SET counter = counter + 1
		(1 mark for incrementing counter)
		
		UNTL counter = length(competitors[]) OR found = True
		(1 mark for loop conditions)
			4

9.	(a)	Any two from the following: • No typing is required to input data. • Restricted choice eliminates possible errors by the user • All the choices are clearly presented to the user • The screen in uncluttered with minimal information.	2
	(b)	Vegetarian	1
10.		Hybrid (as part of the storage can be accessed by the public while the remaining storage is only accessible, privately, by the company)	1
11.		If the company expands quickly (obtains several new large contracts to sell tickets) it must be able to cope with sudden increases in the number of users accessing their website (1 mark).	1

Section 2

Question		Expected Answer(s)	Max mark
1.	(a)	Only the names of the molecules need be stored (1 mark). The Number of H atoms and Chemical Formula can be generated from the number entered by the user and therefore do not require to be stored (1 mark).	2

Question			Expected Answer(s)	Max mark
	(b)	(i)	Twos Complement (1 mark) The left hand bit of the number is used to store its equivalent negative value (eg −128) (1 mark). **OR** Signed Bit (1 mark) The left hand bit is used to store whether the number is negative or positive (1 mark).	2
		(ii)	Twos Complement – Range from −128 (1 mark) to 127 (1 mark) **OR** Signed Bit – Range from −127 (1 mark) to 127 (1 mark)	2
		(iii)	As there can never be a negative amount of something (in this case carbon atoms) it is unnecessary to store negative numbers.	1
	(c)		(Stepwise) refinement	1
	(d)		SEND numberOfCarbonAtoms*2+2 TO DISPLAY 1 mark for calculation using an appropriate variable name. 1 mark for output to screen.	2
	(e)	(i)	Reference – the data type is passed into the subroutine, modified and passed back out.	1
		(ii)	Procedural	1
	(f)		A breakpoint is used to pause the program at a selected line of code (1 mark). At this point the values currently stored in variables and data structures can be compared with expected results (1 mark).	2
	(g)		Perfective	1
2.	(a)		Entity Relationship (diagram)	1
	(b)		Many birds live in the one habitat (1 mark). A single type of bird may live in more than one habitat (1 mark).	2
	(c)		Any one from the following: (1 mark each) • Bird's Latin Name • Habitat Name • Insect's Latin Name Each of the above fields are string data types (1 mark).	2
	(d)	(i)	By installing multiple web servers, each web server is capable of hosting multiple websites (1 mark). Each virtual server can be tailored to the customers' needs (1 mark).	2

Question			Expected Answer(s)	Max mark
		(ii)	*Any two from the following:*	1
			• Scripting may be used to validate data entered into web forms.	
			• Queries may be initiated by web pages and subsequently carried out using scripting languages.	
			• Scripting languages are used to format selected data in a web page and return it to a browser in the form of an HTML page.	
	(e)		Note that this is quite an open question, which allows for many possible ways of answering the question. It is important that answers relate both to the scenario and to rights/responsibilities of the users/owners of the website.	2
			For example:	
			The website owners are legally responsible for the content of the website (including blog comments) and must monitor the comments (1 mark).	
			The website owners should not remove comments because they simply disagree with them as they could be accused of stifling users' freedom of speech (1 mark).	
3.	(a)	(i)	**Advantages:**	2
			• More secure (harder to hack code or bypass validation completely)	
			• Improved compatibility (client does not need to have a scripting language installed/enabled)	
			Disadvantages:	
			• Can increase network traffic as requires more calls to and replies from the server	
			• Responses to user may be slow and frustrating in scenarios where bandwidth is poor	
		(ii)	Each meter reading would be stored using a record structure (1 mark).	3
			Description or diagram of the four variables required within each record and their data types (name – string, accountNumber – integer, meterReading – real, dateOfReading – integer). Complete for 2 marks, 1 or 2 mistakes for 1 mark.	
		(iii)	To comprehensively test the scenario would require testing using multiple examples (1 mark) of:	4
			Normal data	
			Extreme data	
			Exceptional data (all three for 2 marks)	
			In addition the response time of the server should be tested to ensure that the user only waits for an acceptable time (1 mark).	

Question			Expected Answer(s)	Max mark
	(b)	(i)	Error – Line 5, < should be > (1 mark)	2
			A meter reading must be higher than the previous reading so can never be less than 0 so the condition in line 5 can never be met (1 mark).	
		(ii)	SET finalCost to (lastYearsReading – thisYearsReading) * unitPrice	3
			SEND ["Your bill for this year is" & finalCost] TO DISPLAY	
			(1 mark for subtraction in brackets, variables must be in order shown	
			1 mark for multiplying by unitPrice	
			1 mark for suitable concatenated message using variable from line 11)	
4.	(a)		One advantage and disadvantage from each list for 1 mark each:	4
			Proprietary Software	
			Advantages:	
			• Guaranteed support available if software fails	
			• Software is well tested and bug/virus free	
			• Software is easy to install and use	
			• Free updates are often provided to user	
			Disadvantages:	
			• Software requires that single or multiple user licences are purchased	
			• Users have no say over facilities within the software	
			• Newer versions of the software may have to be purchased following operating system updates	
			Open Source Software	
			Advantages:	
			• Software is free	
			• Software is being updated/improved continually	
			• User is not locked into using other systems that are often required by proprietary software	
			• User can adapt/edit software as they wish	
			Disadvantages:	
			• Often less user friendly than proprietary software	
			• May be developed along lines of developers interests rather than user's needs	
			• Code is open to other users who may be able to exploit vulnerabilities in the software	
			• There may be hidden costs such as external support	
			• Less official support than proprietary software as support provided by the developers/users community	

Question			Expected Answer(s)	Max mark
	(b)		Spyware is software that aids in gathering information about a user without their knowledge (1 mark). The software may send such information to another party (1 mark).	2
	(c)		Abubakar can encrypt the file using Jill's public key (1 mark). Jill can then unencrypt the file using her own private key (1 mark).	2
5.	(a)		A wire-frame diagram contains the framework of a document/website such as position of content, navigation, layout details etc. while noting little of the documents actual content.	1
	(b)		*Any two from the following:* • Developers have a clear idea of what they are producing so little discussion/hesitation required • Design decisions are clearer therefore require less revisiting/tweaks later • The developer and client are both clear about what is being produced reducing the number of meetings required and possible changes that may result	2
	(c)		*Any two from the following:* • Drop-down menu system • Scrolling images in left hand panel • Shopping Basket	2
	(d)		ID's or Classes may be used to define a style that can then be applied to any tag.	1
	(e)	(i)	Agile	1
		(ii)	*Any two from the following:* • The garden centre will quickly see working parts of the website • The garden centre can make late changes to their requirements • The completed website will be delivered faster	2
		(iii)	User Interface decisions should be made early (1 mark) and implemented by each team through the use of templates (1 mark) and cascading style sheets (1 mark).	3
6.	(a)	(i)	Multiple cores will improve the processing capabilities of the devices (1 mark) allowing for increased complexity (more simultaneous events, better sound, higher resolution) in the applications produced for the devices (1 mark).	2
		(ii)	To make use of multiple cores the operating system software should be capable of processing more than one instruction simultaneously.	1

Question			Expected Answer(s)	Max mark
		(iii)	*One mark for name and one mark for any of the following:* • Reduced power requirements allowing for longer battery life • Increased number of internal registers increasing processing speed • Wider bus widths increasing processing speed	2
	(b)		Applications are written to work with particular operating systems (1 mark). An update to the operating system may require new versions (or patches) to the application (1 mark).	2
	(c)		Bluetooth – Short distance radio wave based system (1 mark). Wi-Fi – Local Area radio wave based system (1 mark). 3G or 4G – A set of standards that make use of the mobile phone telephone network (1 mark).	3

HIGHER FOR CfE COMPUTING SCIENCE MODEL PAPER 3

Section 1

Question			Expected Answer(s)	Max mark
1.			*Any two from the following:* • Bandwidth Consumption – Flood the network connection to the server with traffic, preventing the web server from passing data • Server Memory – Flood the server's memory with data to prevent applications from running efficiently • CPU Usage – Force the server to run processes that prevent it carrying out its normal tasks • Hard Disk Space – Copy data to the server's hard disk drive until you prevent it being able to save data • Database Space – prevent databases used by the server from saving data	1
2.			Run length encoding relies on the graphic containing many pixels of the same colour in a row (1 mark). In a graphic with 32 bit colour depth it is unlikely that many two adjacent pixels will be exactly the same colour (1 mark).	2
3.			Solid state drives have a significantly faster access speed than hard disk drives (1 mark). **OR** Solid state drives are more robust as they have no moving parts (1 mark).	1
4.			Working –	2

	numberOne	numberTwo
Initial values	5	10

The program loops three times, each time updating the value stored in numberTwo and then storing twice this value in numberOne.

	numberOne	numberTwo
After first pass through loop	30	15
After second pass through loop	90	45
After third pass through loop	270	135

numberOne = 270 (1 mark)
numberTwo = 135 (1 mark)

Question			Expected Answer(s)	Max mark
5.			Adaptive maintenance	1
6.			Signed bit (1 mark) – 10010010 Two's complement (1 mark) – 11011110	2

Question			Expected Answer(s)	Max mark
7.			The control unit will activate the read line to transfer the instruction (1 mark). The control unit supplies the clock signal by which the events are coordinated (1 mark).	2
8.			*Any two from the following:* • Alpha testing takes place in house while beta testing takes place externally, often on the customer's own systems • Alpha testing is carried out by the developers or an independent test team whereas beta testing is carried out by the potential customers • Alpha testing focusses on finding errors (bugs) in the code whereas beta testing focusses on ensuring the product works in situ	2
9.	(a)		As each section of the program is completed the team will design the next section.	1
	(b)		Increased emphasis on design will ensure code is written with fewer errors (1 mark) which will lead to fewer rewrites of code following testing (1 mark).	2
10.			Digital certificate	1
11.			Under the Regulation of Investigatory Powers Act (1 mark) the company must supply a government authority with encryption keys if they are required as part of an investigation (1 mark).	2

Section 2

Question			Expected Answer(s)	Max mark
1.	(a)	(i)	Unallocated memory = Total amount of available memory – Allocated memory Unallocated memory = (2 x 8Gb) – (587Mb + 480Mb + 60Mb + 1.5Gb) Unallocated memory = (2 x 8192Mb) – (587Mb + 480Mb + 60Mb + 1536Mb) Unallocated memory = (16,384Mb) – (2663Mb) Unallocated memory = 13,721Mb Unallocated memory = 13.4Gb 1 mark for assigning values to the formula (line 2 above) 1 mark for converting all values to the same units 1 mark for final answer, in Gigabytes	3
		(ii)	Memory Management	1
	(b)	(i)	Ross should take regular copies (1 mark) of files and store them in a separate location (1 mark).	2
		(ii)	Many cloud providers will offer free antivirus protection as part of their service.	1

Question			Expected Answer(s)	Max mark
	(c)	(i)	The rival author has broken the Computer Misuse Act (1 mark) by accessing Ross' computer system without his permission (1 mark). He also broke the Copyright Designs & Patents Act (1 mark) when he copied Ross' work and published it as his own (1 mark).	4
		(ii)	*Any two from the following:* • Use encryption to protect the content of his files • Password protect the files or the location they are stored in • Use biometric security to prevent access to his computer system	2
	(d)		The upload speed of the users Internet connection	1
2.	(a)	(i)	 In a relational database entities with one to one relationships would be created using a single table. (1 mark)	5
		(ii)	Wood ID – Forest table or Order table (1 mark) Customer ID – Order table (1 mark)	2
	(b)		A composite key (1 mark) should be added as it is possible that the Forest Name or Location may not be unique (1 mark).	2

Question			Expected Answer(s)	Max mark
	(c)		Create a query (1 mark) with the following fields: Customers.Customers Name and criteria = "Bespoke Kitchens Limited" (1 mark). Order Table.Order ID, Wood Types Table.Wood Name, Wood Types Table. Price per ton & Order.Tonnes Ordered (all 4 fields for 1 mark). Calculate the Total Cost from the Price Per Tonne and Tonnes Ordered fields (1 mark).	4
	(d)		Boolean	1
	(e)		*Any one from the following:* • A syntax error could occur if a query was incorrectly formatted • A syntax error could occur when using a formula to perform a calculation • A syntax error could occur when a validation rule is incorrectly entered	1
3.	(a)	(i)	The navigation bar along the top uses the style (1 mark). Any two from the following for the remaining two marks: Each of the headings is centred within its own area. text-align: center (1 mark). The text is white. color: white (1 mark). The text is all upper case. text-transform: capatalize (1 mark).	3
		(ii)	24 bit	1
	(b)		<html> declares the text in the tag to be html code (1 mark). <head> includes a title for the document, and may include scripts, styles and meta information (1 mark). <title> contains the text that will appear at the top of the browsers window (1 mark). <body> contains the content of the web page (1 mark).	4
	(c)	(i)	Interframe compression saves key frames at set periods (1 mark). Between the keyframes only the difference between the frames is saved (1 mark).	2
		(ii)	A lossless file may be uncompressed, recreating the original file with all the original data (1 mark). When a lossy file is compressed the data is permanently lost (1 mark).	2

Question		Expected Answer(s)	Max mark
	(d)	*Any two from the following:* • Alternative text for images – allows text readers to inform blind users on the content of the image • Keyboard input – allows users who struggle with mouse use to use the website • Transcripts of audio files – to allow hearing impaired users to access audio content • Label the Structure of the page – this allows users who can only access part of the page at a time to know they are looking at a new section • Colour selection – avoiding colours that cause problems for colour blind users improves accessibility • There may be many other answers to this question so use your own judgement when marking your answer	2
4.	(a)	Main Memory – slowest type of memory but has largest storage capacity (1 mark). Cache – faster than main memory but stores less data (1 mark). Registers – fastest access but only small amounts of storage (1 mark).	3
	(b)	*Any two from the following:* • Increased internal bus width – improves the number of bits the CPU can process simultaneously • Increased external bus width – improves the number of bits that can be received simultaneously by the CPU • Increased cache (level 1 & 2) – allows more instructions to be stored near or within the CPU increasing processing speed • Multi-core processors – multiple cores allow the simultaneous processing of more than one instruction • Reduced instruction set (RISC) – simplifying the CPU instructions allows them to be processed faster	2
	(c)	The width of the data bus determines the number of bits that may be stored in each memory address (1 mark). The width of the address bus determines the number of possible addresses in memory (1 mark). The total amount of memory is determined by the number of addresses multiplied by the size of each address (1 mark).	3
	(d)	The manufacture (1 mark) and disposal (1 mark) of a component also create a carbon footprint during the lifetime of the component.	2

Question		Expected Answer(s)	Max mark
5.	(a)	The height of the hill was recorded to the nearest foot meaning there are no real numbers stored in the file only integers.	1
	(b)	*Any one from the following:* • The program may not be able to locate the file • The file may have no data to read • The program may attempt to read beyond the end of the file • The data in the file may be in the wrong order leading to the program attempting to store a value in the wrong data type (for example a string into an integer data type) • The data may be stored in a format unreadable by the program	1
	(c)	A record structure could be used (1 mark) to store a string and integer for each hill (1 mark).	2
	(d)	The file management system locates the file in backing storage (1 mark). The input/output system transfers the data into memory (1 mark). The memory management system allocates memory address for the data to be stored in (1 mark).	3
	(e)	Arithmetic Logic Unit	1

Question			Expected Answer(s)	Max mark

(f)			If you have written your answer using a programming language match each line to one of the pseudocode answers below.
			
			Solution 1
			(Use Find Max algorithm to find highest hill and store name of hill at the same time)
			
			SET maxHillheight TO hillHeight[0]
			SET maxHillName TO hillName[0]
			　　　　　(1 mark for first two lines)
			
			FOR counter FROM 1 TO length(hillHeight)　　　(1 mark)
			
			　IF hillHeight[counter] > maxHillheight THEN　　(1 mark)
			
			　　SET maxHillheight TO hillHeight[counter]　(1 mark)
			
			　　SET maxHillName TO hillName[counter]　　(1 mark)
			
			　END IF
			END FOR
			
			SEND ["The highest hill climbed is" & maxHillName] TO DISPLAY　(1 mark)
			
			Solution 2
			(Use Find Max algorithm to find highest hill and store the position of the maximum value in the array)
			
			SET maxHillheight TO hillHeight[0]
			SET position TO 0]
			　　　　　(1 mark for first two lines)
			
			FOR counter FROM 1 TO length (hillHeight)　　　(1 mark)
			
			　IF hillHeight[counter] > maxHillheight THEN　　(1 mark)
			
			　　SET maxHillheight TO hillHeight[counter]　(1 mark)
			
			　　SET position TO counter
			　　　　　　　(1 mark)
			
			　END IF
			END FOR
			
			SEND ["The highest hill climbed is" & maxHillName[position]] TO DISPLAY
			　　　　　　　(1 mark)
				6

(g)	(i)		Count Occurrences	1
	(ii)		Value (1 mark) The array is passed into the subroutine and is not altered when the program counts the number of hills over 3000 (1 mark).	2

HIGHER FOR CfE COMPUTING SCIENCE 2015

Section 1

Question			Expected Answer(s)	Max mark
1.			1000 1000 – using 8 bit 2's complement method **OR** 1111 1000 – using sign bit method	1
2.	(a)		Many to many	1
	(b)		One to one	1
3.			Jimmy 0 Jimmy 3 1 mark for Jimmy output twice Or 1 mark for Jimmy 0 Or 1 mark for Jimmy 3 2 marks for full correct answer	2
4.			Feature • Rule • Uses capital letter to identify variables to allow for instantiation Benefits • Adds information/meaning based on other facts/rules • Reduces need for repetition of facts/rules or improves efficiency by reducing code • Facilitates queries • Use of variables allow values to be returned • Any other valid *Any 2 bullets – 1 mark each*	2
5.			• (Provide facilities) for public authorities (e.g. police/MI5/government) to intercept electronic communications • fit equipment to facilitate surveillance (technical services) • pay for systems to assist with interception of electronic communications • pay for the hardware needed to store electronic communication • inform staff of the fact that access to communication data is subject to the RIPA *1 mark for each bullet, maximum 2 marks.*	2
6.	(a)		• Date • Time • Script attached to interface item	1
	(b)		• Recommended items • Name	1
7.			1 mark for correct simple condition found = true/counter = 49 2 marks for correct complex condition found = true OR counter = 49	2

Question			Expected Answer(s)	Max mark
8.			*Any two of the following:* • Allows the client to see/test/ feedback on proposed solutions • Subsystems/specific elements can be prioritised and tested as early as possible • A range of proposed solutions can be developed on a small scale instead of the need for full implementation	2
9.			*Any two of the following:* • Frequently accessed data/ instructions are held in cache • Faster access memory (on the same chip as processor) • Reducing the need to access slower main memory	2
10.			*Any two of the following:* • End user group/independent test group (1 mark) • Given tasks to perform/observed performing tasks (1 mark) • To provide feedback/evaluate (ease of use/fit for purpose) (1 mark)	2
11.			A primary key with more than one field (or attribute or column).	1

Section 2

Question		Expected Answer(s)	Max mark
12.	(a)	Order no, Item ID	1
	(b)	• Customer to Order + Item to Sale + Order to Sale all related and no others • Two of above three are the correct 1:M • All three above are the correct 1:M *1 mark for each bullet.* *Many representations are possible.* Customer ⤙ Order ⤙ Sale Sale ⤛ Item	3
	(c)	Customer.Customer name Customer.Customer address Item.Description Item.Cost Order.Order no (or Sale.Order no) Order.Date Sale.Quantity [Order no]=10728 • Award 1 mark for all four tables (Customer, Item, Order, Sale) • Award 1 mark seven correct fields • Award 1 mark for criteria of [order no] = 10728.	3

Question		Expected Answer(s)	Max mark
	(d)	SUM([Sale.Quantity]*[Item.Cost]) and is placed in the Report Footer • Use of SUM or clear description • Quantity*Item cost used or clear description • Report Footer or Summary field	3
13.	(a)	• Specific processes/instructions/ tasks can be allocated to certain processors/core processors (1 mark) • Allowing concurrent/simultaneous execution (of scripts and different media elements) (1 mark)	2
	(b)	Use of RLE • Stores the colour of a pixel and • the number of repetitions of the pixel • Reducing the number of pixel values stored Use of JPEG • Takes shades of colour and stores them as one colour • Which can then be stored as a pixel value and number of repetitions Use of LZW • Uses an algorithm to identify patterns • Assigns each pattern a pointer value • Reducing number of pixel values stored MPEG • Stores (key) frames • (Key) frames saved as JPEG • Delta frames save changes between key frames Any other valid. *Any combination of bullet points stated for a maximum of three marks.*	3
	(c)	Create a web based app rather than a native app (1 mark). And any one of the following: This can then be viewed using any browser (regardless of OS) (1 mark). So that there is no need to install an app (on an OS) (1 mark).	2
	(d)	• Encryption is used (to encode the e-mail) • Keys are used to encode or decode data • A public key is used to encrypt/A private key is used to decrypt the data	3
	(e)	• To prevent keylogging • To prevent brute force attacks *Either bullet for one mark.*	1

Question		Expected Answer(s)	Max mark
14.	(a)	boolean	1
	(b)	This is one approach to solving this problem. **Reference Language** Line 1. SET valid TO True Line 2. IF Length (mobile_number) <> 11 THEN Line 3. SET valid TO False Line 4. ELSE Line 5. FOR counter FROM 1 TO 11 DO Line 6. IF (Mid(mobile_number, counter, 1) < "0") OR (Mid(mobile_number, counter, 1) > "9") THEN Line 7. SET valid TO False Line 8. END IF Line 9. END FOR Line 10. END IF • 1 mark for checking the length of the string • 1 mark for using a loop to traverse over each character • 1 mark for use of a correct complex if or loop condition (may include check on first character being zero) An additional mark may be awarded for any of the following bullets for a maximum of two marks. • 1 mark for use of conditional loop that includes a request for re-entry of mobile number • 1 mark for valid use of a Boolean ◦ 1 mark for an error message if an invalid number has been entered	5
	(c)	• Name of a valid parameter AND passed by reference/byRef (1 mark) • As the value will be updated AND returned/passed out (1 mark)	2
	(d) (i)	A hybrid cloud is a combination of a private and public cloud (1 mark).	1
	(ii)	*Any two of the following:* • Store sensitive data on the private cloud (1 mark) • Can outsource services to public cloud (at times of need) (1 mark) • Can easily expand capacity of public cloud storage without hardware costs (1 mark) • Public cloud use will not results in the purchase of new hardware/servers • Public cloud use reduces cost in relation to backup strategies (1 mark)	2
15.	(a)	• Use an emulator (to imitate the older operating system) • Virtual machine • Compatibility mode	1

Question		Expected Answer(s)	Max mark
	(b)	*Any two of the following:* • Different groups/profiles • Different rights/permissions • Set up a public folder	2
(c)	(i)	• <u>Data format conversion</u>/converting camera signals eg serial to parallel. • <u>Buffering/temporary storage of data</u> in transit between the camera and the computer/compensates for differences in speed between the camera and the computer. • <u>Handling of status signals</u>/to ensure camera data is received correctly. • <u>Voltage conversion</u>/to change voltage levels of the camera to relevant levels for the computer. • <u>Protocol conversion</u>/ensure camera and computer adhere to the same protocols. *1 mark for each statement of 2 different functions – maximum 2 marks.* *Question is a 'state' and so underlined terms on their own are acceptable but any valid description is acceptable.*	2
	(ii)	*Any two of the following:* Bit-Map • Bit mapped graphics can be edited in fine detail at pixel level • More realistic images • Less constrained by mathematical objects Vector • Objects can be layered • Scalable without losing resolution/no pixilation • Editing individual attributes	2
(d)		$90 \times 25 \times 260 \times 200 \times 24$ = 334.7 MB • 1 mark for 1st line – different expressions are acceptable • 1 mark for final answer Fully worked response: $90 \times 25 \times 260 \times 200 \times 24$ = 2,808,000,000 bits = 351,000,000 bytes = 342773.4375 KB = 334.73 MB = 334.7 MB	2
(e)	(i)	Advantage: • reduces the need for computers/parts to go to landfill • Reduces amount of potentially toxic waste • Any other valid	1
	(ii)	Advantage: • Newer computers are built to high environmental standards • use less power/less carbon footprint • Any other valid	1

Question		Expected Answer(s)	Max mark
16.	(a)	An internal style sheet is embedded within the HTML code for each page (1 mark) whereas an external style sheet is a separate file (that can be used by multiple pages) (1 mark).	2
	(b)	*Any two of the following:* • An external style sheet would be loaded once and (cached locally for future use) (1 mark) • Internal style sheets would be downloaded every time the page is viewed again (1 mark) • Webpages have larger file sizes due to the embedded internal style sheets which take longer to download (1 mark)	2
	(c)	<link rel = "stylesheet" type= "text/css" href= "masterstyle.css">	2
	(d)	H1 {font-family:Tahoma; color:blue; text-align:center} • H1 (or H2) with { } • font-family:Tahoma; • color:blue; • text-align:center *1 mark for each bullet for a maximum of three marks.*	3
	(e)	• Make use of a keywords meta tag (to include the terms 'Glasburgh Safari' or 'pandas') (1 mark) • Make use of terms 'Glasburgh Safari' or 'pandas' throughout the body of the pages of the website • Include keywords e.g. ('Glasburgh Safari' or 'pandas') in the title tags (1 mark) • ALT tags on images • Create/submit a sitemap • Any other valid	2
	(f)	A query could be used to calculate how many tickets are available (1 mark). An appropriate message is generated from the result of the query (code is used to generate a message) (1 mark).	2

Question			Expected Answer(s)	Max mark
17.	(a)	(i)	• Assigns values to (element one of) an array • Assigns values to the Test_mark record *1 mark each, maximum of 2 marks.*	2
		(ii)	89	1
		(iii)	SET average TO (pupil[1].mark_1 + pupil[1].mark_2 + pupil[1].mark_3)/3 • 1 mark for logical average with assignment • 1 mark for reference to the variable pupil at least once	2
	(b)	(i)	2	1
		(ii)	Logic error	1
		(iii)	• Line 3 needs changed • FOR counter FROM 0 TO 3 DO	2
	(c)		A – 74.33 B – 1 C – 57.67	3
	(d)		• Stop/pause program at a defined point • to check the values of the variables (match the expected value)	2

Acknowledgements

Permission has been sought from all relevant copyright holders and Hodder Gibson is grateful for the use of the following:

Eric Isselee/Shutterstock.com (SQP Section 2 page 17);
Bill Bertram (Own work) [CC BY-SA 2.5 (http://creativecommons.org/licenses/by-sa/2.5)], via Wikimedia Commons (http://upload.wikimedia.org/wikipedia/commons/3/33/ZXSpectrum48k.jpg) (Model Paper 1 Section 2 page 8);
unclepodger/Fotolia (Model Paper 1 Section 2 page 10);
Boris Ryaposov/Fotolia (Model Paper 1 Section 2 page 11);
B. Wylezich/Fotolia (Model Paper 1 Section 2 page 14);
Luap Vision/Fotolia (Model Paper 1 Section 2 page 19);
Luap Vision/Fotolia (Model Paper 1 Section 2 page 19);
Africa Studio/Fotolia (Model Paper 1 Section 2 page 19);
roger ashford/Fotolia (Model Paper 1 Section 2 page 19);
Elnur/Fotolia (Model Paper 1 Section 2 page 19);
Ivonne Wierink/Fotolia (Model Paper 1 Section 2 page 19);
Can Yesil/Fotolia (Model Paper 1 Section 2 page 21);
Nataly-Nete/Fotolia (Model Paper 1 Section 2 page 21);
pumppump/Fotolia (Model Paper 2 Section 1 page 2);
Viktor Gmyria/Fotolia (Model Paper 2 Section 2 page 11);
Volodymyr Khodaryev/Fotolia (Model Paper 2 Section 2 page 19);
kingan/Fotolia (Model Paper 3 Section 2 page 8);
guysagne/Fotolia (Model Paper 3 Section 2 page 11);
guysagne/Fotolia (Model Paper 3 Section 2 page 11);
savcoco/Fotolia (Model Paper 3 Section 2 page 11);
stockphoto-graf/Fotolia (Model Paper 3 Section 2 page 11);
andreacionti/Fotolia (Model Paper 3 Section 2 page 11);
Andrey Semenov/iStock/Thinkstock/Getty Images (Model Paper 3 Section 2 page 11);
GoodDween123/Shutterstock.com (2015 Section 2 page 10).

Hodder Gibson would like to thank SQA for use of any past exam questions that may have been used in model papers, whether amended or in original form.